CW00544696

The Rule of Law
And Other Essays

The Rule of Law

And Other Essays

Kenneth Jupp

SHEPHEARD-WALWYN (PUBLISHERS) LTD

© Kenneth Jupp 2005

All rights reserved. No part of this book may be
reproduced in any form without the written permission
of the publisher, Shepheard-Walwyn (Publishers) Ltd

First published in 2005 by
Shepheard-Walwyn (Publishers) Ltd
Suite 604, The Chandlery
50 Westminster Bridge Road
London SE1 7QY

British Library Cataloguing in Publication Data
A catalogue record of this book
is available from the British Library

ISBN-13: 978-0-85683-235-2
ISBN-10: 0-85683-235-9

Typeset by Alacrity,
Banwell Castle, Weston-super-Mare
Printed through Print Solutions, Wallington, Surrey

Contents

Publishers' Note

THE AUTHOR sadly died before the book was published. The publishers wish to thank his widow, Lady Jupp, and family for their help. Their thanks are also due to Richard Barnes for a careful revision of the manuscript, to L.L. Blake for helpful advice and to Jean Desebrock for her careful editing and indexing. A final word of thanks to Kenneth Dunjohn for his Foreword.

Foreword

Our Very Learned Friend!

IN HIS 1956 book, *Adventure in Search of a Creed*, F.C. Happold described his attempts to provide a new and innovative way for school-boys (and girls) to look at and think about the great questions of the world. His guidance, essentially for sixth-formers, ranged over physical science, history, philosophy, theology and psychology. It was objective inquiry and took in the great questions that all with a searching mind might pursue over the meaning of life and our origins. Happold was clearly a remarkable teacher and his series of penetratingly informative books have helped many a seeker find a spiritual path.

The special relevance here is that Sir Kenneth Jupp, author of the remarkable essays which follow, had the good fortune to have Happold as his house master at Perse, his school in Cambridge. Only days before his illness took a terminal turn, Kenneth talked about Happold – to be exact, more in terms of the swimming trips on the river, but with sweet and warm memories of a man who had first kindled the light of explor-ation in the young Jupp mind. It was at Perse, too, that Kenneth began, and was able to indulge, what became his lifelong love of the classics. So here we begin to have a hint of an explanation for an astonishing enthusiasm and innovative mind that were Kenneth's, and which were destined to enrich the lives of his beloved family and the many, many friends who sat enthralled by his brilliant forays into history, coupled with deeply objective analyses of the present.

Kenneth Jupp, born 1917, was one of five brothers. His father was a ship broker, his mother a musician. From Perse, he won a scholarship to University College, Oxford and there consummated his romance with language and the ancients. It was not all study. A love of rowing was a constant preoccupation though, despite this, Kenneth was awarded a First in 1938 and the College prize for Greek a year later. A career in the law was mooted but World War Two intervened. Already aware of the Nazism that was menacing Europe, Kenneth had joined the Territorial Army, was commissioned and was one of the first to be mobilised, and very soon despatched to France as a gunnery officer with the Royal Artillery.

In 1940 he was part of the evacuation from Dunkirk. His next action was in North Africa and later, in early 1944, he was in the amphibious attack at Anzio, as the Allies invaded Italy. It was in this brutal battle that Kenneth, slight, shortish but full of pluck and daring, then a forward observation gunnery officer in support of the advancing 6th Battalion, Gordon Highlanders, found himself attacked and his unit overrun. And here there is another characteristic of the Kenneth Jupp so many came to know. Largely alone, his communications disabled by a bust wireless, he was way out ahead of the main troops, planning, plotting targets and trajectories, and then taking part in a fierce counter-attack that ended with him using his talents and his extraordinary courage to assist in the evacuation of wounded. He was hit in the leg himself and had to be hospitalised back to UK – but not before being gazetted for a Military Cross.

In the Army hospital in Britain, hours of tedious rest were more than this bristling intelligence could handle so, from his bed, Kenneth enrolled with a correspondence course and pursued his law studies. Once recovered, he was appointed to a war office selection board, tasked with helping select the Army's future officers. Later he was posted back to Italy – and, with combat easing down, and conforming to his norm of never wasting an opportunity, he signed up for singing lessons in Naples. No wonder that as his life progressed music played so huge a part – Kenneth would break into song at almost any provocation: a light, rich voice ranging from lilting ballads, through Mozart arias, to jolly extracts from Gilbert and Sullivan.

War over, Kenneth began his law career in seriousness and he joined Lincoln's Inn and was called to the Bar in 1945. In 1947, he married his beloved Betty and four young Jupps emerged over the years. He was never happier than when joined with all of his lovely, talented family, which later included a bevy of grandchildren.

Here, then, we have a mind dedicated to the law, cultivated to pursue the classics, and with a curiosity keen to probe the fundamental questions of knowledge; all this encapsulated with courage, determination and a sparky, innovative talent. And a facility for being ahead of his time.

But that still does not enable us to discover how it was that Kenneth came to be, for many who followed his thinking closely, an icon of understanding in economics and in matters spiritual – to be, in fact, a fountain from whom treasures freely flowed.

Around the century's midpoint, Betty Jupp resolved to take an interest in a possible new career and was exploring the requirements of the examinations for the Institute of Chartered Secretaries and Administrators. An economics paper would be part of the test. Aha! Kenneth had seen advertisements on the London Underground for lectures in economics and he resolved to take a course at the Suffolk Street headquarters to see if the content would be helpful to Betty's exam aspirations. He quickly determined it was not what the chartered institute would find suitable. But Kenneth had realised he was hearing truths about a subject so many encrusted with mere data and unproven theory. It was here that the name Henry George began to arouse his questing talents. This American economist's writings, notably *Progress and Poverty*, overturned many of the shibboleths of conventional economics – and appealed to Kenneth as they seemed to penetrate to what is basic in an understanding of human relationships. It was not long before he was himself teaching the precepts of his new understanding and, interestingly, one was never long in his company at an event in later years before someone approached to say, 'You were my first tutor!' And how cherished for so many were those weeks at Kenneth's lectures where economics had become alive. The key question he now faced was how was it that, despite decades of magnificent technological advance, vast multitudes, even in the developed world, remained in poverty? It was this deeply felt concern that seems to have spurred Kenneth for the rest of his life.

He struck out in a brief sojourn with politics, standing in the Liberal interest at North Hendon in the 1951 general election. It was where we first met. In neighbouring South Hendon, one of the leaders of the Suffolk Street school, Leon MacLaren, stood similarly for the Liberals. But it was the party's lowest ebb: most of their candidates lost their deposits and the pair in Hendon, despite huge help from students, registered the lowest ever Liberal votes in the two divisions. So it was back to the economics studies.

Then, several years later, taking the cue from the Henry George view that philosophy would need to be understood to establish the ultimate truth in economics, the Jupp scene was elevated by the teachings of P.D. Ouspensky, a Russian writer and teacher whose works were read and followed all over the world. Love of wisdom and the need to be in the present moment became key concepts, and along with the teaching was a practical exercise designed to enhance the experience of awareness. For Kenneth it became an integral part of his life, even to the very end. And his special moment for practising it was at the kitchen sink, doing the washing up. Indeed, the Jupp household never acquired a dishwasher – 'I'm the dishwasher,' Kenneth would say, and he was. And he did it unvaryingly with attention.

In recent years, many of the formative strands in Kenneth's life began to come together. None surprised him more than when this writer was able to show him a connection between George and Ouspensky! The latter was a correspondent for *New Age*, a journal edited in London by A.R. Orage, and in a 1919 article he berates the criminal element in post-revolutionary Russia and cites George's remarks in *Progress and Poverty* that our civilisation does not require any foreign barbarians for its destruction, carrying within itself its own barbarians who might destroy it (*Letters from Russia*, Routledge & Kegan Paul, 1919, page 37). The sentiments, though provocative, need not trouble us, but the connection should, and as far as it is possible to surmise it seems that Leo Tolstoy was the link. He was an associate of Ouspensky and admirer of George.

Early in the 1960s, contact was made with leaders of India's principal holy tradition, *advaita*, one of the important developments being the introduction of a system of meditation. Some will recall Monday 13 March 1961 when the slim, smartly suited figure of Kenneth stood alongside the Maharishi Mahesh Yogi, in white and gold flowing robes and seated on a doe skin, in the vast space of the Royal Albert Hall, where nearly 5,000 were eager to hear about the wisdom emanating from the Himalayas. Kenneth was chairman of the event and characteristically dealt firmly and deftly with the proceedings, even the few hecklers. For him it was an especially poignant moment for his late mother had played the organ in that great hall.

Meditation became a key part of Kenneth's life and the family say he was repeating his mantra virtually to the end. His spiritual interest turned increasingly to the words of Shantanand Saraswati, Shankaracharya of Jyotir Math in India, whose discourses with the late Dr Francis Roles and other members of the Study Society were his constant companion in later years.

Professionally, Kenneth's successful Bar practice led to his taking Silk in 1966, first predominantly in criminal law and personal injuries but moving swiftly on to parliamentary work. He became a Recorder in 1972 and three years later was appointed a High Court Judge, sitting in Queen's Bench Division, and for four years as the presiding judge on the north-eastern circuit. Lincoln's Inn Bencher, Sir Mervyn Davies MC, who spoke so movingly at Kenneth's memorial service, described him as a judge who was 'firm and fair'. *The Times* said he was 'modest, courteous'. His law career spanned the chairmanship of numerous tribunals and official bodies and he played a part in hearing appeals in Northern Ireland at the height of the security problems. There were numerous special moments in his judgements, notably when he declined to grant damages to a mother suing a health authority for the failure of a sterilisation operation.* He retired in 1990.

So far we have been largely discussing the skeletal aspects of a most distinguished life. What of the man himself, the inner or essential man? What, indeed, has given rise to the profound and penetrating essays that comprise this posthumous book? It was a passion – a huge, huge passion. It was his search for truth in divine, natural and human law. This is what led him to an immediate appreciation of the laws applying to land, as first expounded by George, to the principles of *sanatan dharma* to be found in the teachings of *advaita*, to the wisdom prevalent in the writings of ancient Greece, and, perhaps most of all, to the essential truths that comprise Old Testament teaching and New Testament gospels. In an article written for the Study Society he tells us that the concept of natural law predates even Greek philosophy and first emerged in Sanskrit teachings in the Code of Manu. And *dharma*,

---

* His reasons are given in the Appendix, p.139.

Kenneth argues in that article, is best translated as 'the best way to live'.

Kenneth had come to realise that most, if not all, truly sacred writings can be received at two levels, with inner and outer meanings, and that behind the words can be found layers of import and implication evident only to those with an eye and mind to seek for fundamental realities. To take the example of what was an abiding and tenacious search for the truth in a sacred sentence, Kenneth had almost always in his mind the words of the Gospel of John: 'In the beginning was the Word, and the Word was with God ...' What is the meaning within meaning, what flows from this?

Here the focus turns to his further great study and passion, that of language. To help get at truth, he explored words to a depth that made him an authority not only in English, Latin and Greek but also in Sanskrit and Hebrew – plus German and a touch of Gaelic, too. This was the nature of this remarkable man: go to original sources and if that required deep study, so be it. The essays of the book are chock-full of original sources and encompass so much of his acquired knowledge and understanding that only the most careful reading will reveal the power of the many insights Kenneth has bequeathed to all whose minds are open.

With passing years, his explorations grew in depth and in understanding. Whilst esoteric ideas, economics and spirituality clearly comprised the material from which this man was made, there were other aspects, too. What started out as simple, conversational journeys with Kenneth on almost any subject rapidly became enriching adventures. His encyclopaedic knowledge, and astonishing memory, illumined the intellect, warmed the heart and stimulated one's own little grey cells. So many facets to this man! Impeccable good humour; great fun; instinctive love for life – he survived numerous cardiac procedures and major operations, and even came through several weeks in a coma. When his angina was rampant, he trekked to Russia where, by invitation, he lectured to the *Duma* on the essentials of land reform! His kindness and warm-heartedness were boundless, seen notably in his great loyalty to friends. There was a time when a particular associate had financial problems and Kenneth sought to auction some of his own book collection to help out! He worked tirelessly for the organisations he supported – he was a patron of the St James schools, and a trustee of the Land Research Trust and its one-time chairman.

What then of this book itself? To describe it as broad-ranging is an understatement. Near the beginning comes a learned discussion of Genesis, the formation of the earth and how the Creator made man in his own image; and within a few lines our attention is directed to problems associated with 3G, the very latest in mobile phones, and government systems of licensing for them. Swiftly moving on, we are exposed to the ozone layer and the ionosphere. And then Kenneth's observation: 'Man did not bring himself here.'

There will be many who pass judgement: it is an exhaustive dive into the realms of justice – or is it injustice? He penetrates beyond the superficial and tackles questions of enormous proportions, all the time reverting to scriptural teachings from biblical and related sources and also from the classics and from his own special, innovative, path-finding mind. These are essays to ponder, to relish and to have as the basis for a reflective study of where this modern world has reached in terms of the happiness of man. As the pages are turned, Kenneth's words should be kept in mind: 'The challenge of the twenty-first century is how to establish access to the resources of the earth for the whole population so that the able-bodied can support themselves. The welfare state can then be slimmed down to no more than is needed to provide for the diseased and disabled. These constitute only a small minority and could then be provided for with more generosity than at present.' A manifesto for a political movement?

To come full circle, F.C. Happold, at the conclusion of his book *Religious Faith and 20th Century Man* (Penguin Books, 1966) tells a story of a Zen Buddhist novice who asked the master of the monastery for spiritual instruction. 'You have had your breakfast?' asked the master. 'Yes,' replied the novice. 'Then', said the master, 'go and wash the dishes.'

Concludes Happold: 'It all sounds very simple, too simple to be true. Yet when in interior recollection, selflessness, and desire – and the desire is everything – men have followed the path of what is for them the equivalent of washing the dishes, they have in the end found the hidden treasure.'

Kenneth found the treasure. His greatest desire was to be able to share it with all.

As you embark on the journey that Sir Kenneth Jupp MC would have

you follow, reflect on the closing words of the oration at his memorial
service at Lincoln's Inn: 'It is sufficient now to say that Kenneth stood
as a model for what a man should be!'

KENNETH DUNJOHN

Introduction

Searching for Justice

WHERE IS JUSTICE to be found? This collection of essays sets out on the same quest as Plato's *Republic* but from a point in time more than two thousand years later. There are many people today who have good reason to complain of injustice. The media find no difficulty in reporting injustices every day of the week. In the chapters which follow, we examine seven facets of life which many people tend to blame as responsible for the lack of justice in today's world – seven areas of life in which injustice is easily discovered. Yet it is justice for which we are searching.

Each essay takes a different theme

- **1 *The Nation State*** 'Why do the nations so furiously rage together?' What is it that binds people together? Is it the nation state? In order to be free from constant warfare should we be persuaded to abandon our national sovereignty? Ought we to come under the control of a wider organisation such as the European Union, or a United States of Europe, or even a United Nations world government? Could the nations be kept at peace by an over-riding framework of international law?

- **2 *Economic and Political Freedom and Forms of Government*** Does the fault lie with the forms of government adopted by different nations? To what extent is their social organisation, their division into classes, their insistence on armaments, the balance they strike, or fail to strike, between freedom and security, to blame for the national and international disorder of today?

- **3 *The Rule of Law*** This is often referred to today with great approval. But what does it mean? Is it different from natural law?

Whose law is the rule of law? Edmund Burke said, 'There is but one law for all, namely, that law which governs all law – the law of our Creator, the law of humanity, justice, equity, the law of nature, and of nations.'* The rule of law is more than just the imposition by the powerful on the less powerful of a system of law that suits them. Can a universal rule of law applicable to all and recognised by all take the place of the complicated and contradictory systems of national law which exist today?

- **4 *Philosophy, Science and Religion*** – the threefold division of learning. Is science in conflict with religion? Can philosophy bridge the gap between them? Does religion act as a divisive force, pitting all religions against each other? Can there be a brotherhood of man in a world of multiple religions?

- **5 *Money*** has for long been suspected of being a corrupting influence. Is love of money the root of all evil? Why, say some, should banks be allowed to create money? Should money and banks come under greater surveillance? There are many enthusiasts for monetary reform. But are they aiming at the right target?

- **6** Does the fault lie in ***capitalism*** itself, as is nowadays a growing belief amongst many? What really is capitalism? Is it the same thing as money?

- **7 *Conclusion:*** 'Justice standeth afar off.' Is socialism the culprit? There is no doubt that socialism has lost the immense appeal it achieved after the Second World War. Is that an improvement or will it in fact make matters worse? To what principles must a state subscribe if it is to find justice?

Or is the search for justice in vain? Is justice to be found anywhere in this world of ours? There are glimpses of justice to be seen – in nations, in government, in law, in philosophy, in science and religion, in money and banking, in capitalism and in socialism. We need only eyes to see it and love to bring it to birth and give it expression.

Without love (by which I mean Greek *agape*, brotherly love, charity,

---

* Impeachment of Warren Hastings.

generosity), knowledge is narrow, limited and incomplete. As love increases, knowledge also goes on increasing. Our emotions can confirm truth for us and give us direct perception of deeper truth. Too often, however, negative emotions can also block the direct perception of truth. How then can we purify ourselves sufficiently, raise our sights and our work to be always open to the glory of creation?

Dante's Vision – The Universal Law

> *La Gloria di colui chi tutto move*
> *Per l'universo penetra, e risplende*
> *In una parte piu, e meno altrove.*

The glory of Him who moveth all things, permeates the universe,
and shines now here, now there, with greater or less splendour.

This was the vision that met Dante's eye when, in the third book of his *Divine Comedy* he was finally led into paradise by Beatrice, the symbol of love. In the two previous books he had been guided by Virgil (symbolising human reason and study) to describe in journalistic form, albeit in verse and using allegory, the Hell and the Purgatory of life in the Italy of his time. Dante's poetic insight contains a great truth which could change our vision of what justice is and how it might truly be found. It underlies much that is written in the following pages.

Prologue

'In the beginning God...'

WHEN THE White Rabbit asked where he should begin, the King of Hearts said gravely: 'Begin at the beginning and go on to the end: then stop.' This is good sense. In searching for justice, one must begin at the beginning, and refer back continually to the First Cause, the Absolute Beginning, the Source.

In mediaeval universities the seven subjects covered by the trivium and the quadrivium (the three 'ways' and the four 'ways') were considered to be the key to universal learning. In the centuries since the Renaissance the scientific age has fragmented these seven ways into a number of parts, and added many entirely new studies to the list. Altogether there is now a plethora of subjects, most of which claim to make a scientific approach to the matter in hand. But the scientific approach usually implies deliberately detaching the subject from its metaphysical aspect. Science deals with material things. But there are things beyond the five senses. From a so-called 'scientific' point of view the First Cause has to be left out. The unfortunate result has been that incomplete arguments have frequently been constructed to reach incomplete conclusions.[1]

Religion uses 'God' to denote the First Cause. Etymologically, 'God' only means the object of our worship, whatever that may in fact be. And it may take many forms. Some make Wealth their God. Others worship Position, or Prestige, or Rank, and seek it avidly. Worshippers of Power occur only too frequently in history, devastating whole continents in their search for conquest. Napoleon and Hitler are only the last of a string of such. These gods must certainly be kept out of the argument. Unless one

---

1   Einstein said, 'Science without religion is lame. Religion without science is blind.'

goes back to the first cause of all things – call Him the Creator, the Almighty, the Absolute, the Root, the unknown God, the Source – logical argument must remain relative, and in consequence any conclusion to the argument must be only relatively sound. Inevitably this brings us to the story of creation and the Old Testament, the early books of which contain the Western world's recollection in myth, tradition and memory of the early history of mankind. The first five books, the Torah, are hallowed by Jews, Christians and Muslims alike.[2]

Man on Earth

The Book of Genesis describes how the planet Earth was formed, and relates how the Creator made man in his own image, and gave him dominion over the Earth and all its creatures. The human race was enjoined to 'be fruitful, and multiply, and replenish the earth and subdue it'.[3] The Book of Genesis may not be literal history, but can there be any doubt that, as a poetic description of the process of creation by and from the source of the whole of the universe, including man and the creation of man's unique role of stewardship within the universe, Genesis conveys an essential truth. The same essential truth lies at the heart of every tradition's creation myth. Man did not bring himself here.

Mankind's success in subduing 'the earth' has brought about considerable changes in the meaning of the word. A couple of centuries ago it would have been sufficient to describe how man lives by referring to his making use of the earth's mineral, vegetable and animal life. These were the source of all his wealth, vital to his survival. Today we have to stress a number of important minerals – oil in particular – as well as earth's hydrosphere, atmosphere and outer space. These include the beneficent ozone layer, which we are said to be gradually destroying, and the ionosphere, which, with satellites in outer space, has now been found useful for deflecting and directing radio waves, thereby immensely extending our means of communication. Those seeking to profit by controlling them have, in recent auctions for 3G licences, demonstrated their immense value. Billions of pounds were paid for the monopoly of their use. These modern developments show the extent to which man has

---

2   This remarkable fact tends to be overlooked today, when these three religions seem to be locked in conflict. How they share the Torah of our Old Testament is described in Chapter 7.
3   Genesis 1:26 and 28.

been able to carry out the biblical command to 'subdue' the earth. But in so doing he has ignored the concomitant command to 'replenish the earth'. All the sons of Adam have wasted, polluted and destroyed much of the earth entrusted to them. 'Green' parties in various countries are now drawing attention to how destructive mankind has been. International conferences, attempting from time to time to deal with the problem, have so far had little success.

Food-Gatherers

Man began as a food-gatherer, and accordingly could inhabit only those few favoured parts of the earth which were well-watered, prolific in natural growth from which he could gather food and drink, and which had sufficient materials for the very little clothing and shelter necessary in such places. In this paradise mankind remained very close to the Divine. He saw the Creator immanent in all things. The God who sustained him was his life and his livelihood. What he ate and drank was God. He needed no mass or eucharist to remind him of that. But very few of the earth's vast resources were available to him. He was confined in blissful ignorance to the tiny fruitful areas in warm climates, exemplified in the book of Genesis by the Garden of Eden – probably Mesopotamia between the two rivers Tigris and Euphrates. Trouble began only after he had eaten 'the fruit of the knowledge of good and evil'.

Nimrod, Cain and Abel

He learnt how to hunt, tame and herd animal species, and even to domesticate certain of them. Nimrod, 'the mighty hunter', helped to extend the limits of human dominion into inhospitable areas where only wild creatures could live and find food. The hunter could feed on the flesh of his prey, and clothe himself with their hides. Abel was a keeper of sheep, which could survive in areas where man on his own could not. Sheep needing to graze over large areas of otherwise inhospitable land increased the areas of the earth the herdsmen could occupy while tending them. Their flesh provided food and their wool could be used for clothing.

Agriculture and Settled Land

A revolutionary change in the history of man took place when he began to cultivate the soil to produce crops. The importance of this change must be emphasised. It became essential for him to exclude others from the land he tilled, so that he could reap the harvest of what he had sown. The farmer could not have the hunter or the herdsman and his animals treading down the young crops. He had to enclose the field. Thus of the sons of Adam, Abel was a keeper of sheep while Cain was a tiller of the ground. The result of their quarrel 'when they were in the field' was murder; and this has been reflected in land disputes in most of the countries of the world where agriculturists have settled. They bore the mark of Cain upon them. Unable to convince the aboriginal native inhabitants of their need to have permanent possession of land, they have in most countries resorted to force, and made war on the natives in order to seize and retain land. The aftermath of this conflict remains to this day among the tribes of many continents. What has happened to justice here?

Europeans and Aboriginal Tribes

The difficulty was that, while the hunter and the herdsman roamed over large areas, chasing their prey or obtaining fodder for their animals, the cultivator of the soil had of necessity to enclose his field to protect the growing crops. 'What is produced by my labour is mine by right.' The harvest is his by reason of his labour. He must therefore, if he is to reap what he has sown, exclude others from his field. Land enclosure is essential to an agricultural society. The hunters and herdsmen are necessarily displaced from the lands over which they were accustomed to roam. So, in modern times, invading from Europe, the heirs of Cain have displaced, and where necessary slaughtered, native tribes in America, Maoris in New Zealand and Aborigines in Australia who are even now claiming compensation for their lost tribal lands. Some, most notably today in Zimbabwe, are reciprocating with destruction of property, torture and murder.

Land enclosure (in Scotland 'clearances') has been the subject of argument between historians from time to time over the last two or three centuries. The biblical account has the merit of going to the heart of the question.

The Importance of Land

Whatever stage of culture mankind may have reached, land is a vital necessity to every human being. He must have land on which to live, and land from which to gain access to the riches of the earth, and to the society of his fellow human beings. The food-gatherer depends on land no less than does the farmer, and as urban societies develop they still need land for houses, for factories, for shops, for offices and for much else, and no less than any purely agricultural society.

It is therefore not surprising that throughout history seizures of land have been the cause of wars. From earliest times lack of access to the use of land (whether because one is literally driven off it or because the new owner who has seized it demands access fees – rent – which cannot be easily afforded) – has been the chief cause of poverty. Some relief has been afforded by emigration to new lands or even a New World. Following the departure of the Romans, Germanic and Scandinavian tribes invaded Britain in search of new lands. America was peopled by Europeans seeking free land. Elsewhere in the world new territories were settled and new nations founded, sometimes peaceably, but usually by force of arms. In mediaeval times the poor and the dispossessed were supported by charity, largely through the Church. The Tudor Poor Law used local taxation (the Poor Rates) to support the landless. Finally in the twentieth century the public conscience compelled governments to levy national taxation to support the poor and so a welfare state was born. The taxation needed for this purpose has grown and keeps on growing. But the poor in fact continue to remain poor. More recently international organisations such as the European Union and the International Monetary Fund have adopted the same strategy of taxing the rich nations to support the poor nations. In the EU, for example, the Common Agricultural and Fisheries Policies are intended to pass the wealth of the richer nations to those less well developed. Unfortunately both systems are very wasteful. In some instances rich as well as poor take advantage of the benefits of the system. Much of the money is absorbed by the costs of administration. Not a little of it disappears into the pockets of fraudulent individual claimants, and in the case of poor nations into the pockets of their corrupt governing classes. Moreover, as a proportion of income, the taxation to sustain the system in practice falls far more heavily on the poorer taxpayer than on the rich. It is self-defeating. In the welfare state the poor continue to fare poorly. Now and again they try to rise up in revolt, only to be crushed again and set back in their place. What has happened to justice here?

England During the Commonwealth

It was in seventeenth-century Britain that writers came to recognise the importance of land. Both John Locke (1632-1704) in England and Viscount Stair (1619-95) in Scotland cited biblical authority that 'the Almighty gave the earth and all that is therein to mankind in common for the support and comfort of their being'.[4] Even without biblical authority it was abundantly clear that there is no other source from which a man can acquire food, clothing and shelter. In his physical nature man is a land animal, utterly dependent on the resources of the planet earth, on the dry surface of which he lives. He has to maintain eventual contact with land, even when he navigates the seas, or the skies, or the vastness of space. In order to live at all, each of a nation's families has to have space on land within the nation's territory on which to dwell, from which to make use of the resources of the earth (running water, fuel etc) and from which to engage in some productive work. It follows that at all stages of man's development land must be available to all. Landlessness is a prime cause of injustice.

Man and Society

But land is by no means all. Mankind was created a social animal. Families naturally gather into clans, clans into tribes and tribes into nations. Food-gatherers, hunters and herdsman alike looked to a chieftain, who was usually descended from, or recognised as representing, the tribal patriarch. Under his leadership they defended areas of territory, making war if necessary, or, if better advised, avoiding contact with other tribes in the wide spaces then available, as did Abraham and Lot when they returned with their cattle out of Egypt.[5]

The agricultural way of life gave a great impetus to the formation of both smaller and larger societies. Individuals and families naturally combined their strength and their wits to increase the earth's powers of production. By trading, they stimulated production still more. Each

---

4   James Dalrymple, Viscount Stair's famous *Institutes of the Law of Scotland.*
5   Genesis 13:5ff.

produced only those things which suited him and his land best, and then obtained the whole variety of other things he needed by exchanging his products for what others produced. Families gathered into villages where the farrier, the blacksmith, the wheelwright took over time-consuming tasks which they, as specialists, could perform more swiftly, more skilfully and more cheaply than the farmers themselves. The miller ground corn into flour for them all, while the grocer shopped collectively for the whole village. In time villages grew into towns, where shops were more specialised, and some towns enlarged into even more specialised and sophisticated cities. For example, the City of Leicester became a centre of the English leather goods industry.

In these stages of expansion a new antagonism made its appearance. The miller, the shopkeeper and other village or town specialists were usually a good deal richer than the farmers. Many a folk song celebrated the fact. City dwellers were wealthiest of all. They were making less and less direct use of the earth's bounty in animal, vegetable and mineral products, and increasingly making use of contact with their fellow human beings (e.g. buying and selling) and finishing what others had made. The produce of the earth came to them indirectly through other people.

Earth's most potent source of wealth is the combination of human beings in co-operation. The industries that this creates bring an increase in wealth far exceeding what can be earned by tending the herds, tilling the soil or extracting the minerals lying beneath it. Great wealth depends on a concentration of people. Cybernetics – systems of control and communication – are of immense value in this. From the pony express postal system, established in the vast empire of Genghis Khan eight centuries ago, to the internet of today, there has been a progressive linking together of mankind by methods of communication.

The art of printing allowed thousands to read simultaneously the writing of one. By the end of the fifteenth century it had spread all over Europe. The seventeenth century saw the beginning of the scientific age, which demonstrated the power of human co-operation. Canals and turnpikes with fast stagecoaches were speeding up transport and travel. Primitive types of semaphore signalling followed in the eighteenth century, railways and steamships in the nineteenth century; motor vehicles and aeroplanes, telephones and telegraphs in the twentieth. And now cyberspace.

War and Peace

Yet war has almost always been the habitual occupation of the nation states and their leaders. At the beginning of the seventeenth century wars all over Europe had reached such epidemic proportions as to shock informed opinion. The suffering experienced in central Europe was immense. Accordingly, when the Thirty Years War was brought to an end in 1648 by the Peace of Westphalia, Hugo Grotius's work *On the Law of War and Peace*, published during the conflict, began to be studied. It established the notion that *international law*, based on the theoretical equality of individual nations, could put an end to war by protecting the weaker against the stronger nations.

International Law

International law recognised that title to unoccupied land could be established by discovery, so long as discovery was followed by effective occupation. Prior to its discovery a land was regarded as *res nullius* ('no thing'). The chequered history of the Falkland Islands, discovered and partially settled at various times by French, British and Spanish expeditions, demonstrates the contentions that can arise over this doctrine.

Many lands were in fact already occupied by savage tribes. But international law regarded these as having no international status or personality. The difficulties besetting this doctrine are illustrated by the fate of the native tribes of North and South America, and the aboriginal tribes of Australia and elsewhere. If these had been taken into account, then it would be true to say that only a small part of the territory acquired by the world's nations has been obtained by discovery. Nearly all of the rest has been acquired by conquest. International law has always recognised conquest as a valid root of title, so long as any earlier occupants have been sufficiently vanquished and crushed to be powerless to reclaim the land.

Following the growing acceptance of international law, treaties between nations kept them at peace, and various nations formed themselves into groups in order to maintain a balance of power. This system lasted into the twentieth century. But its precepts did not avail to prevent the horror of Napoleon's conquests. After Waterloo the Congress of Vienna set the scene for general European peace over the next hundred years, but it still did not stop Bismarck's invasion of France and the Prussian occupation of Paris in the Franco-Prussian War of 1870-1.

Then in 1914 war on an unprecedented scale broke out. The weapons included machine guns, explosive shells, tanks and poison gas. The casualties on land and at sea were enormous. They included large numbers of civilians.

International Organisations

The peace of 1918 resulted in the formation in 1920 of the League of Nations, which was supposed to stop nations from attacking one another. However, it had no army, and could do nothing to stop Italy from conquering Ethiopia in 1935. The League collapsed with the rise of Hitler and the outbreak of the Second World War, which ended with the dropping of atomic bombs – terrifying weapons which caused greater death and destruction than had any weapon hitherto. After the war the League was resurrected in the form of the United Nations Organisation, which was again designed to find peaceful solutions to international problems. The post-war years were dominated by the rivalry between the American and Russian blocs, both extensively armed with nuclear weapons of ever greater destructive power. In the late 1980s the Russian bloc dissolved and America was left as the sole superpower.

The European Union

Other attempts at international co-operation had also been made. Geneva Conventions in 1864, 1906, 1929 and 1949 tried, not always successfully, to improve the treatment of prisoners of war. A number of special organisations to control health, agriculture, trade, fishing, the environment and so on were made either by treaty or under UN auspices. The most recent and, for Europeans, most important of the former is the European Union. It arose out of the Second World War, has grown in size, wealth and influence steadily and quietly, and is now a major force to be reckoned with in taking over the powers formerly exercised by national governments. As yet it has no armed forces except such as it pleases the member nations to provide. Its government is by no means directly representative of the individuals in all the member nations. By no stretch of imagination can it yet be described as democratic. So what in fact is it? It does not fit into any of the well known categories of government to be described below. It is more than a customs union but less than a nation state. It appears to be run largely by a civil service answerable only to a Council of Ministers from its member nations, who meet infrequently. As has often happened, such a civil service can easily become the master of those it is supposed to serve. If there is to be an overall government of Europe, the vital question is on what permanent settlement are the powers of government to be divided between the central 'European' government and the member nation states.

National Independence

One of the chief difficulties in forming and holding together a government overarching a group of nations is the lack of cohesion of the people it encompasses. The links which bind people together into a nation are very much stronger than the differences that separate them. Today there is as much centrifugal force splitting nations apart – for example in the United Kingdom, which now boasts three, and at times four, separate parliaments – as there is centripetal force trying to unite nations together under a European government. Meanwhile Yugoslavia and some parts of Russia have been torn apart by separatists.

Still at the Beginning

We started with God, the source of all creatures, believers and non-believers alike. We find ourselves now in times of change and uncertainty searching for better, more just ways to rule ourselves. To whom will we turn? Where is justice in the sphere of international relations?

1

The Making of a Nation

THE DICTIONARY definition of a Nation is: 'a large number of *people* of mainly common descent, language, history, etc, usually inhabiting a *territory* bounded by defined limits and forming a society under one *government*.'[6]

People

MEN AND WOMEN vary enormously: strong or weak, tall or short, intelligent or stupid, active or passive, spirited or lethargic – these are only some of the differences, with gradations of many kinds between the two extremes of each category. The list is long and detailed. Nevertheless, religion and philosophy the world over recognise a broad threefold distinction between those in whom physique, emotion or intellect predominates.[7] This is not surprising, since the human body is traditionally divided into head, heart and physical prowess. Of course mankind has all three attributes: it is simply a matter of where, because of unequal development, the balance lies. Accordingly, in the division of labour between individuals, a nation is comprised of three broad classes, defined by their preference for work of a physical, an intellectual or an emotional nature.[8]

Common Descent
The human child, unlike the young of most other species, takes a long time to come to maturity. For many years the growing baby, child and

6   *Concise Oxford Dictionary*, 1976.
7   Cf. the Bible story of Martha and Mary, the laws of Manu, Plato's *Republic* etc.
8   See also the quotation from Alfred the Great, below p.20.

youth depends for nourishment and protection on parents or near relatives. This makes the family, rather than the individual, the natural unit from which a nation is formed.[9] The word 'nation' (from the Latin *natio*) implies a connection by birth. In small societies, 'common descent' usually covers the blood-related families who have joined together in a tribe or clan with only a few outsiders who may have been adopted into the enlarged families. But the adoptions can be very remarkable.

In fact the composition of a nation is far more complicated than this. There must be some people in England today, for example, who, without knowing it, are descended from the union of a Roman legionary and an ancient Briton – perhaps a slave, perhaps a free woman, by marriage or otherwise. The legionary could have been conscripted into the Roman army from almost anywhere in the Empire. Many of the later Roman Emperors were not in the least Roman by blood. In the nations of central Europe, the possibilities of the mixture of races – Huns, Goths, Visigoths, Vandals, Aluns – are enormous. The United States today is in itself a remarkable conjunction of diverse races – 'nations' in its etymological sense.

The United Kingdom

If we take Britain as an example, we see that the mingling of races is remarkably diverse. The aboriginal inhabitants during the stone and bronze ages are conveniently but misleadingly referred to as 'Iberian'. In fact they were of more widespread origins than that name suggests. They included not only peoples from the western European seaboard, but also men of Mediterranean and Alpine stock, probably attracted by the rich deposits of tin and copper in southern and western Britain which they needed for smelting bronze. These were no mean people but rather a force to be reckoned with. This is evident when one stands before Stonehenge in awe, wondering how they found it possible to build like that, and to fetch some of the vast stones from a hundred miles away. The historian G.M. Trevelyan may be going a little too far in saying that some 'Iberian' blood probably flows in the veins of every modern Englishman, more in the average Scot, most in the Welsh and Irish.[10] But that some such blood is in many of us is indisputable.

9   See H.J.S. Maine, *Ancient Law*, London, John Murray, 10th edn, 1906, p.270 and *passim*.
10 G.M. Trevelyan, *History of England*, London, Longmans, Green & Co, 3rd edn, 1945, p.7.

The Celtic Strain

The Celts who succeeded them were a far more coherent race, although by no means amicably united: quite the reverse. But they are recognisably of one descent: tall, fair or red-haired, eyes of green or light blue, a distinct blood group, with abundant hair of which they were very proud.[11]

Much of Britain was thoroughly Romanised in the first four centuries of the Christian era. But the Roman features – square heads with dark hair – to be seen among the French population, particularly in the valley of the lower Rhône, are rarely seen in English faces. There must have been some Romans who settled, and many more who fathered children on the Celto/Iberian female population of Britain, but the influences left by the Roman occupation were more of a historical and cultural kind.

The Northern Tribes

The Germanic and Scandinavian contribution to our blood is the most far-reaching. The Saxons came in during the Roman occupation, but only after the Romans had left did the tide of invasion, and sometimes of peaceable settlement, flood in. Danish and Norwegian (Viking) invasions followed, with each wave of invaders turning for the most part to resist the next comers, until in the ninth and tenth centuries the country settled into a more or less 'English' conglomeration of tribes: Jutish in the extreme south; Saxon further north and west; Anglian in the east and, going further north, Danish (in Lincolnshire and Yorkshire), and Norwegian in southern Scotland and all round the Scottish coasts and the islands of the Orcades and Hebrides. The Celts had meanwhile been pushed to the borders of Scotland and England, and into some of the mountainous parts beyond, where they mingled with the Iberians.

The Norsemen

It was this heterogeneous population that the Duke of Normandy conquered and melded into one. He had come with yet another host of

11 This is how the Roman writers, particularly Julius Caesar, described them. They can be seen today on the borders of Wales, and in Scotland. One could see them at Paddington Station some years ago coming off the GWR train from Gobowen, which used to serve the Welsh border country near Oswestry and Welshpool: a woman with six red-headed children, and two of their uncles, one six foot seven, the other six foot four tall. As Trevelyan points out, most of the dark mountain folk of Wales and Scotland although called, and calling themselves, Celts are in fact Iberian.

Vikings who (the traditional date is AD 911) had been allowed by the King of West Frankia to settle in what is now Normandy. By 1066 they had adopted Frankish ways and spoke their own special kind of French. They brought with them a large number of adventurers from many other parts of Europe, and were followed by Jews. The latter kept themselves to themselves, but the Normans increased the Viking blood in the existing mixture. It is not without interest that the eighteenth-century Comptroller-General of France, Turgot (etymologically *Thor-God*), whom we quote in later pages, is paralleled in the Domesday book by a family of the same name who were landowners in Lincolnshire before the Conquest, and one of whom, as Archdeacon of Durham, had the remains of St Cuthbert moved into Durham cathedral.

There were many other minor injections of new blood into England in modern times: Dutch, Huguenot, Jewish; and now all sorts of colours and creeds from the former British Empire and elsewhere. Many have come for refuge from tyrannical governments in many parts of the world. In tracing descent in this country, there could hardly be a more varied field.

Language

A common language binds together a far larger group of families, some related, some not. It is often an amalgam of the languages of conquerors and conquered. English is largely derived from the languages of Celtic, Latin, Saxon and Norman French invaders of this island, flavoured with a sprinkling of words from other incomers. The Romany language of the Gypsies gave us the word *pal*; *smashing* comes from the Gaelic phrase *'s math sinn* ('tis good, that): these are but two unusual and delightful examples.

The strong influence of Latin on the English language contrasts with the paucity of Roman blood traits in the English. This was emphasised throughout Britain when, at the end of the sixth century, long after the Romans had withdrawn, St Augustine founded the Roman version of Christianity in Kent, and became the first Archbishop of Canterbury. Latin then became the religious language, not only of the English, but also of some of the so-called Celtic regions of Britain. The names of officers of the Church – *rector*, *vicar*, *deacon* – are of Latin origin, in both English and Gaelic.

With the Conquest, Norman French became the language of the Court, the nobility, and the law, with Latin still in use by churchmen and for important documents. Edward III was the first king of England to learn English, Henry VII the first to speak it as his native tongue. But the astonishing thing is that, although English was banished for two and a half centuries to be used only by the peasantry, when it did revive it swept the board. Its revival was largely due to the hatred of all things French at the time of the battles of Crécy, Sluys and Poitiers. In due course English became the recognised common language of the whole of the United Kingdom, and hence of the heterogeneous population of the USA. It now bids fair to stretch its linguistic kingdom over the whole of Europe as a second language. Those who resist it in the Celtic fringe are, alas, a very small minority. It is no exaggeration to say that the language of England is one of the most potent forces binding together people of east and west, north and south.

History
Common history is a binding force which brings in a large number of people who have no apparent connection by birth. The limited etymological meaning of 'nation' (from Latin *natus*), already weakened, then virtually disappears. North America provides an outstanding example. No matter how diverse their origins, Americans share a history of having fled from the troubles of the Old World to find a new life in the vast expanses of a whole new continent. It is a bond between them.

Not until after the Spanish Armada was destroyed and Spanish sea power had been overcome in Elizabeth's reign did it became safe to colonise what was to become the United States. But in the seventeenth century emigration to America offered escape from religious persecution, from the pressure of the state, and from landlessness, with many of the earliest immigrants coming from the highly populated eastern counties of England.

Religion
One of the strongest historical influences to be reckoned with is religion. In some parts of the world there are bitter divisions, both between nations and within nations, which stem almost entirely from the religion which for historical reasons families have adopted or been compelled to adopt.

Religious persecution in Europe was a strong influence driving people to seek a new life in the vast spaces of America. But the settlers in the American states themselves often persecuted other settlers who happened to follow a different religion. The Puritan Pilgrim Fathers colonised Massachusetts, and repeated religious persecution drove some of them on to other parts of New England. Pennsylvania was colonised by Quakers, Maryland by Roman Catholics. To these in the eighteenth century were added German and Irish refugees, including some Protestant Northern Irish. Ultimately, America became the Mecca for people fleeing from all parts of Europe in search of land and a better life. But it needed the War of Independence, and the Civil War, to cement Americans into a nation.

Territory

THE WEALTH of a nation depends upon its natural resources. In an entirely agricultural community, this is a matter predominately of climate, fertility, water resources and the like. In highly developed urban communities, however, it means the press of people in crowded cities, where the territory is so highly valued that it is bought or rented by the square foot. Some nations have dropped their agriculture in order to develop banking, lucrative financial and other service industries. The quality of life is often higher in a rural setting than in a throbbing Hong Kong type of city where people live at close quarters in skyscrapers, with no gardens and little contact with nature except by means of a long car drive. But in material terms the busy city affords greater wealth to some; to others it brings greater poverty.

Diversity of Land and People

The advantages of land differ from place to place in a nation's territory. One could say that the diversity of people is as great as the diversity of their territory. One of the problems of politics is to match the people with their land. The nations differ just as much as the kind of territory they inhabit. Because of its climate and fertility, Britain was a prime target for invasion by Germanic and Scandinavian tribes in days when the prevailing way of life was agricultural. Nations seeking to extend their territory have for long been one of the chief causes of war. Ethnic, linguistic, cultural and, above all, religious differences have served to foster hatred and to strengthen the morale of the armies on either side of the conflict.

Government

IN A STATE of nature, individuals were free to maintain individually the rights given them by natural law. They could protect their persons and their property, restraining and punishing offenders, and exacting reparation for damage done to them. But the difficulty of carrying this into effect is so great that men are ready to join together, to surrender their right of private enforcement to a government of some kind which will enforce the law for them. As Locke puts it:

> The great and chief end, therefore, of men's uniting into common-wealths, and putting themselves under government, is the preservation of their *property* [which Locke defined as their 'lives, liberties, and estates'] to which in the state of nature there are many things wanting.[12]

Government can take many forms. Throughout Europe, after the collapse of the Roman Empire, the feudal system evolved out of the sheer necessity for people to put themselves under the protection of some local strong man. The subsequent history of the European nations varies widely, but they have this in common: the protectors amalgamated, sometimes by conquest, sometimes by dynastic intermarriage, sometimes even by agreement. Usually their constitution was monarchical. Germany, for example, at the close of the fifteenth century, was divided into about 150 sovereign states, governed by kings, princes or 'electors' (because they had a vote in who became the Holy Roman Emperor) or bishops. Their number had by the time of the *National Zollverein* of 1848 been reduced to forty-nine states. Democratic forms of government were a rarity, although they were to be found in Holland, Switzerland and Italy.

The Philosophy of Government

To consider other forms of government we have to go back to the Greek philosophers. The advantages and disadvantages of the different types of constitution were discussed at length by both Plato and Aristotle. In

---

12 John Locke, *Second Treatise of Government*, Oxford, Basil Blackwell, 1966, paragraphs 9, 10 and 124.

his *Statesman* Plato listed six possible types: the first three – monarchy, aristocracy and 'ordered democracy' – were each restrained by the rule of law. If not so constrained, these became tyranny, oligarchy and democracy (which might better be described as mob rule), making six in all.

Aristotle favoured a mixed form of government not unlike the balance of power that prevails in the many countries whose constitutions have Anglo-Saxon roots: Great Britain, the USA, Canada, New Zealand, Australia and others. The balance may be between king, parliament and cabinet; or between judiciary, legislature and executive; or between monarchy (or presidential rule), oligarchy and democracy. What is a feature of them all is the great stress they lay upon the rule of law: the general idea that all are equal before the law and that no one, however high his position in society, is above the law.

The Ideal Government

To these six forms of government Socrates (in Plato's *Republic*) added a seventh, the ideal society ruled not just by a king, but by an enlightened king – one who, having turned from the shadowy cave[13] of this world, had seen the light of the other world, and in it 'the essential Form of Goodness ... the parent of intelligence and truth', without which, Socrates insisted, 'no one can act with wisdom either in his own life or in matters of state'.

The Cave

In the allegory of the cave Plato describes the state of mankind as being like that of men imprisoned in a cave. They have their backs to the light coming in through the tunnel entrance to the cave. Their whole attention is forcibly riveted upon the inner wall which they are facing, onto which light from the entrance is projecting the shadows of objects, people and animals. They cannot see the actual things, which are behind and above them, only their shadows.

In modern terms this suggests a cinema, where the audience's whole attention is captured by images on a screen. They see mountains, buildings, seas, fights, love scenes, religious pageants: some may become

---

13 Plato, *Republic*, 514. Socrates describes the cave allegory as 'a parable to illustrate the degrees in which our nature is enlightened or unenlightened': p.222 in Cornford's translation, Oxford, Clarendon Press, 1941.

affected by what they see, as if it were real. In fact reality is behind them, unseen in the projection room. It may be that Plato's parable of the cave explains the remarkable attention given to actors and television personalities today. They have the headlines; their views are canvassed on all subjects; they are even courted by politicians. 'Show business' has become thoroughly mixed up with the serious vocations of life.

There is no difficulty in interpreting the parable. The figures on the screen are the world revealed by the five physical senses. But this world is an illusion. The true reality is the Absolute,[14] the One Light or Father of Lights,[15] which creates all things. From where else can the manifold images of this world come? Therefore, says Socrates:

> It is no wonder that those who have reached this height are reluctant to manage the affairs of men. Their souls long to spend all their time in that upper world – naturally enough … Nor, again is it strange that one who comes from the contemplation of divine things to the miseries of human life should appear awkward and ridiculous when, with eyes still dazed and not yet accustomed to darkness, he is compelled, in a law court or elsewhere, to dispute about the shadows or images that cast those shadows, and to wrangle over the notions of what is right in the minds of men who have never beheld justice.[16]

It is unlikely that such a person would want to rule; if he did, he would be laughed at by the ignorant. This is why a philosopher king is a virtual impossibility. The best by far of the six poor alternatives, Plato said, would be rule by a monarch under the law; but if there are no such legal restraints then democracy is best.[17] To complete the analogy in terms of a cinema, if one is taken out into the daylight, the sun is temporarily blinding. Yet you would not want to live all your life lit only by the lights of the cinema screen, or to believe it was real.

Alfred the Great

In the millennium and a half of English history, only one of our rulers, the Anglo-Saxon King Alfred, benevolent Christian philosopher, scholarly writer and successful soldier, has been named 'the Great'. It has been said of him that:[18]

---

14 *Good Company*, an anthology of Shantânand Saraswati, London, The Study Society, 1987, pp.27-8.
15 James 1:17.
16 *Republic*, 517, Cornford's translation, p.226.
17 Plato's *Statesman* 294ff, especially 302c.
18 *The Dictionary of National Biography.*

No man recorded in history seems ever to have united so many great and good qualities ... At once captain, lawgiver, saint, and scholar, he devoted himself with a single mind to the welfare of his people in every way ... Alfred has drawn to himself the credit that belongs to many men both earlier and later, and even to the nation itself. Among these 'credits', which are to be found in various writers since Alfred's time, are Trial by Jury, the division of England into Shires, Hundreds, Tithings, and Frankpledge: and above all the 'shameless forgery by Grimwald' which represented Alfred as having founded Oxford University and one of its colleges.[19]

There was no need to distinguish Alfred from other famous personages having the same name, for there were no others. There is in fact no evidence of his being called 'the Great' before the seventeenth century. He was the fourth, but favourite, son of Aethelwulf; one astonishing fact of his life was that he was hallowed by the Pope, apparently as future king of the Saxons, when taken to Rome by his father at the age of twelve. He served each of his three elder brothers faithfully before succeeding to the throne on the death of the third, and there is, strangely, no record of his election and coronation. The question remains unsolved: was this because of the 'hallowing'?

It may be that Alfred came nearest to resembling a philosopher king. His humility, his humanity and his understanding of the art of government are shown in this remarkable self-assessment:

> You know that covetousness and greed for worldly dominion never pleased me overmuch, and that I did not all too greatly desire this earthly rule, but yet I desired tools and material for the work that I was charged to perform ... This then is a king's material and his tools for ruling with, that he has his land fully manned. He must have men who pray, and soldiers, and workmen ... Also this is his material, which he must have for these tools – sustenance for those three orders; and their sustenance consists in land to live on, and gifts, and weapons, and food, and ale, and clothes, and whatever else those three orders require.[20]

This remarkable prescription for good government has much to commend it. Alfred's strength lay in his clearly regarding himself as a

---

19 University College, Oxford celebrated the millennium of its foundation in 1872 with a banquet attended by royalty, and in its chapel prayers are still said each Sunday for the soul of its founder, Alfred. The myth had been put to rest by a lawsuit in the eighteenth century. Would that such admirable traditions were more often respected!

20 L.L. Blake, *Sovereignty: Power beyond Politics*, London, Shepheard-Walwyn, 1988, p.14, citing *English Historical Documents*, Eyre & Spottiswoode, Vol. 1, pp.845-6. Mr Blake gives the whole quotation from which this is extracted. The whole is well worth reading, as is his deliberately challenging book.

servant.[21] How many of our present-day Ministers of State so regard themselves? Yet the very word 'minister' means servant.

So where is justice in the nation state? We have seen that a nation is simply a family writ large, and is in turn but a microcosm of humanity. Humanity itself is the light which powers the shadows and shapes of nations on the cave wall – which over time will come and go. Families and nations must be nurtured but they have no permanent reality. Enduring justice must be found at some more permanent level. Undoubtedly, the form of government and the direction and leadership set by it will set the tone and colour the character of all those who live under its sway.

---

21 Winston Churchill reflected this in his speech in parliament during the War: 'I am your servant, you may dismiss me at your will.'

2

Economic and Political Freedom
and Forms of Government

T HE *CONCISE Oxford Dictionary* defines a constitution as a 'body
of fundamental principles according to which a State or other
organization is governed'. The trinity of people, territory and
government which go to make a nation have to be maintained in
balance. This balance is set when they acquire a constitution and a nation
state is born.

Human life has many aspects. Two of the most important are economic and political freedom. If man enjoys both he has some prospect of
fulfilling his full potential. Without them a man is a slave. But it is not
much good to have one without the other. A man who is well fed but
unable to speak his mind is still a slave. A man who may be free to speak
his mind and campaign for change is still a slave if he cannot get work
and has to depend utterly on others for the chance and opportunity for
work, or for a welfare handout instead because all the land (on which
he might start a business) has already been 'taken' (see below). Justice
cannot be found where freedom is so hamstrung. Real freedom, surely,
cannot be enjoyed unless there is justice for all. In this equation, the form
and quality of government is all-important.

In this essay I look particularly at English, European and American
history and ask why political and economic freedom have so often been
treated differently.

Tribal Societies

IN TRIBAL societies government usually lay in the hands of a chief, either elected or nominated from among the blood relations of a previous chief. The emphasis lay on the connection of birth, tempered by ability.[22]

In clans and tribes living by agriculture, the land usually belonged to the chief,[23] but he held it on trust to ensure that each clansman, or the head of each family, had the means of livelihood from land which he held at the discretion of the chief. In some cases[24] the chief was regarded as holding in fee from God. External defence and internal peace were the chief's responsibility, in support of which the clan would faithfully and without fail answer his call to arms, or assemble to give judgement in internal disputes.[25]

Anglo-Saxon England, so-called, was in Alfred's time a conglomerate of peoples, chiefly Saxons, Angles, Jutes and Frisians, who had amalgamated into tribes under their various leaders, then into kingdoms, reduced in number to seven in the Heptarchy,[26] and finally more or less united under one king. They were skilled agriculturalists who gave the central and southern parts of England their characteristic shape. Some Celts remained among them. Danes predominated later, although even in the period when we had Danish kings (1017-42) we still talk of Anglo-Saxon England.

> Between the end of the Roman government of Britain and the emergence of the earliest English kingdoms there stretches a long period of which the history cannot be written.[27]

> Between these two points stretches a great darkness. The most important page in our national annals is a blank. The chief names of this missing period of history – Hengist, Vortigern, Cerdic, Arthur – may be of real or of imaginary men. All that archaeology and history can do is to indicate – not the date, leaders, landings, and campaigns – but only the general

---

22 The Scots' Tanistry is only one example.
23 Kenneth Jupp, *Stealing Our Land*, London, Othila Press Ltd, 1997, Chapter 2: Natural Law and Tribal Societies.
24 For example the Judaic Torah (*ibid.* p.94, citing Chief Rabbi Hertz) from the Soncino Bible's *Pentateuch and Haftorahs*; and the Scots' law in medieval times (Lord Stair, *The Institutes of the Law of Scotland*, Book 2, Title 1).
25 Cf. the Brehon Law of Celtic Ireland and Scotland, and the Athenian judicial assembly.
26 Kent, Sussex, Wessex, Essex, East Anglia, Middle Anglia (Mercia) and Deira.
27 The opening words of Sir Frank Stenton's masterpiece, *Anglo-Saxon England*, Oxford University Press, 3rd edn, 1971.

character of the warfare that destroyed Roman Britain and gave the land to the English.[28]

Nevertheless, from the sagas of the poets and from a comparison with the later Danish invasions about which much more is known, one can draw a reasonable picture of the earlier Saxon incomers. Some were pirates and marauders, showing an intense loyalty to their leader for the time being, hardy warriors, ready to rape, pillage and destroy. Some were invaders in larger bands loyal to a more permanent leader and ready to settle as soon as they could. Some were settlers from the very beginning, men, women and children ready to brave the dangerous North Sea crossing, intent only upon finding better land for agriculture and a gentler climate than they had experienced in Scandinavia or Northern Germany. The result seems to reveal the characteristics of the English that have attracted refugees ever since – peace-loving, but warlike when roused, keen to establish freedom, devoted to justice and capable of good government. Above all the Anglo-Saxons were adept farmers; once settled they gave the English landscape its mediaeval appearance.

Trevelyan described them as 'a warlike, but not a military people … bloody-minded pirates … and at the same time Pilgrim Fathers'. Certainly, it is in Anglo-Saxon England that the roots of our freedom lie.

Political Freedom

IN THE MILLENNIUM since those days the degree of political freedom achieved in Great Britain has been remarkable. The danger of foreign invasion, which had posed a constant threat to Anglo-Saxon-Danish England, came to an end with the Norman conquest. The crushing burden of the Norman aristocracy was a hard yoke to bear, but it ensured a safe defence of the realm. Over the next three centuries the Normans gradually came to regard themselves as English, and the burden eased. The Great Council, which had at least nominal control over taxation, foreshadowed the summoning of parliaments which was to develop over a further three centuries. The monarchs had to be persuaded that they were subject to the law. The supremacy of parliament was only achieved in the seventeenth century at the cost of a civil war.

28 G.M. Trevelyan, *History of England*, p.33.

Annexation of the three nations on the Celtic fringe was not altogether a success. After much fighting Wales, Ireland and Scotland were joined in a union which was only in part voluntary. Yet the political wisdom of Edward I in proclaiming a Prince of Wales, and the good fortune[29] of having the Scottish King James VI inherit the realm of England and Wales as King James I, made the transition smoother for Wales and Scotland than it ever was for Ireland. Scars of former enmity unfortunately remain to this day in differing degrees.

Revolution

The ousting of James's grandson, James II, in favour of his daughter Mary and his son-in-law William III effected the 'Glorious Revolution' – glorious because it was bloodless except in the subjugation of Ireland, which left stains still to be seen in Northern Ireland today. Its great achievement was to establish the lasting relationship between a constitutional monarchy and the legislative supremacy of parliament. In the eighteenth century Hanoverian Kings inherited the throne. That the first two Georges could not speak English was a blessing in that it enabled a select body of members of parliament to establish cabinet government free from overriding interference by the monarch.

The balance of power to which this gave rise enabled Britain to avoid the neglect of the countryside by the landowning nobility, and their concentration in the capital, which proved so disastrous in France. Large numbers of the English nobility remained resident and genuinely interested in their country estates. Their younger sons sought careers in manufacturing and commerce as well as in the army and navy. The classes became mixed, and Britain was spared the horrors of a revolution on the French pattern. The third Hanoverian king, born and bred in England, was affectionately nicknamed 'Farmer George'. In his reign the country prospered, but little of the prosperity reached the landless. By the end of the eighteenth century radical ideas, often originating in France, were in the air, sowing the seeds of reforming zeal which came to fruition in the early nineteenth century.

---

29 Combined perhaps with the sagacity of Elizabeth in naming him as her successor.

Constitutional Change

The three Reform Acts of the nineteenth century brought about a sweeping constitutional change by enlarging the franchise. Hitherto the vote in parliamentary elections had depended on a property qualification: that is to say a title to property in land. The king or queen in parliament, the sovereign legislative authority, consisted entirely of property owners great and small. The Reform Bills began the process, completed in the twentieth century, of giving the right to vote to the whole adult population. Unfortunately the majority of the newly enfranchised voters were landless. The reform gave them power without responsibility: they lacked the stability which possession of landed property brings. Having nothing of their own to protect, those without property must be forgiven for not troubling too much to protect the property of others. Opposition to the first of the Reform Bills gave rise to very serious public disorder. Much of Bristol went up in flames. A far more effective reform would have been to ensure that every one of the queen's subjects had an interest in land. This would automatically have entitled them to vote.

In the second half of the nineteenth century, with the introduction of public education, the common people were able to take a better-informed view of politics. This had results both good and bad. It assisted Karl Marx in the spread of his revolutionary socialist views, and it allowed the Liberal party to awaken the people to the existence of the monopoly of land, which was held by a minority of individuals. Winston Churchill did more than any other leader to publicise the land monopoly,[30] and the need to end it. He did so whilst at the same time advocating measures, intended to be *pro tempore*, to improve the condition of the poor with state pensions, control working hours in shops, and ensure safety in coal mines. This attempt to deal with the land question culminated in the constitutional crisis of 1910, which deprived the House of Lords of its jurisdiction over money bills. The result was unsatisfactory. The land monopoly was left untouched, while the temporary measures to relieve poverty were made the foundation stone of a socialist system which, after implementation of the National Insurance Act of 1946, was dubbed the 'welfare state'. All political parties ultimately became committed to it and at the end of the twentieth century left it as a millstone hanging round

---

30 See *The People's Rights*, a collection of Churchill's speeches as President of the Board of Trade in 1908-9, London, Hodder & Stoughton, 1910; Cape, 1970.

the neck of a genuinely free society. The challenge of the twenty-first century is how to establish access to the resources of the earth for the whole population so that the able-bodied can support themselves. The welfare state can then be slimmed down to no more than is needed to provide for the diseased and disabled. These constitute only a small minority who could then be provided for with more generosity than at present.

First and Second World Wars
The two disastrous world wars of the twentieth century made strong government an urgent necessity and greatly increased the power of the cabinet and, more recently, the prime minister. This has upset the balance of power. Parliament's control over legislation has been weakened by delegation to ministers who now make Orders in Council which the Commons has insufficient time to scrutinise. Much detailed legislation is never looked at by parliament. The newly accepted power of Brussels to legislate by bureaucratic *fiat* is entirely contrary to centuries of English practice. The danger of losing our freedom to autocratic government has been recurrent throughout history. Britain has been fortunate in overcoming the threat with a good deal less bloodshed than in most other countries. We are now faced by the same danger again. It began with the concentration of power in the cabinet made necessary by the two world wars. This drift of power towards Downing Street has continued in peacetime. The acceptance of legislation, directives and regulations from an enthusiastic Brussels regime with little or no scrutiny by parliament has extended autocratic central government even further.

Economic Freedom

IN ECONOMIC matters the case is very different. As the Roman Empire began to collapse, the migrant pressure from the East forced the people of Europe to seek protection for themselves from external 'barbarian' attack, and consequent internal disorder. Families were ready to commit themselves to anyone who could protect them. When troops were still within call in the district, it was to the Roman commander that the people turned for help. They were prepared to surrender their land to him if he guaranteed to defend them. After the Romans had finally withdrawn, they had to seek protection from some other powerful individual. They became his vassals, holding their land from him subject to conditions of rendering him service, or rent in money or in kind. Thus the feudal system emerged like a phoenix from the ashes of the Roman *dominium*. It was a means of preserving peace in a lawless Europe. Its terms were *commendatio* and *beneficium* – service in return for protection. It resulted in small areas of feudal overlordship which came to be governed in a fashion not very different from that of the clan or tribe described above.

The Nation State

These feudalities later merged to form small principalities or protectorates which in turn merged to form small kingdoms; these again merged or were annexed by conquest to form larger kingdoms. Defence was always of paramount importance, but the ambition and greed of kings or princes were often aimed at annexing more territory, either by fortunate marriages and contrived inheritances or by conquest. Wars to this end were frequent. Indeed war had become an habitual European way of life and remained so even after the main threat from westward migration by the various eastern peoples had faded.

Feudalism in England

In the tribes settling in England after the Romans left, most of the land was held by custom as *folc land*. Apart from slaves, of whom there do not appear to have been many, there was land for everyone. The Saxon kings later began to distribute land to the thegns and others who protected or served them as *boc land,* i.e. land held by charter or 'book', but they did this only with the consent of the witenagemot, the council that advised the king. In the later centuries of Anglo-Saxon settlement, England was in close touch with Continental Europe, and a degree of feudalism grew up. Scandinavian contacts under the Danish kings brought in different traditions of landholding, particularly in central England.[31]

Only after the Norman Conquest did England submit to the full Continental version of feudalism. King William claimed the land of England as his by conquest, and parcelled it out to his supporters and some few

---

31 See F.M. Stenton, *The Free Peasantry of the Northern Danelaw*, Oxford, Clarendon Press, 1969.

others as head tenants in return for homage and military or other service. The process was repeated by tenants and sub-tenants down a line of subinfeudation which produced a pyramidal structure of land tenure throughout the land.

> The partition of England among a foreign aristocracy organised for war was the chief immediate result of the Norman Conquest. After all allowance for the sporadic survival of English landowners and the creation of new holdings for the household servants of great men, the fact remains that an over-whelming majority of the manors described in Domesday Book were held by some form of military tenure. The provision of knights for the king was the first charge upon the baronage of the Norman settlement.[32]

After the Conquest such was the military might of the Crown that England was largely spared from the impact of invasion by land which harassed Europe. Guarded to a great extent by the surrounding seas, its armies were for the next three centuries engaged from time to time in foreign adventures, alternately conquering and then losing Continental lands.

As fortifications and siege instruments became more sophisticated, and wars were conducted further and further afield, the kings had to employ and pay professional soldiers for their overseas adventures. War became increasingly expensive. At home the kings employed and paid professional judges and administrators to carry out the duties formerly discharged by the local feudal lord or tribal chief. Relieved of their military and administrative duties by these new professionals, many of these tenants-in-chief from the Crown – barons or *seigneurs* – were left in possession of lands in return for which they no longer performed any duties or paid any rent, in kind or in money. Ultimately, only some services of an honorific nature survived.

However, vassals or under-tenants remained bound to the tenants-in-chief in service and/or payment for their sub-infeudated lands. By the time Europe emerged from the Middle Ages, nearly all services and rents in kind had been commuted into money. This occurred rather earlier in England than elsewhere. For example, military service due to the king for land distributed after the Conquest was very soon commuted into a money payment of 'scutage'. Money, however, was constantly losing its

32 F.M. Stenton, *Anglo-Saxon England*, p.682.

value, and when the kings tried, as some did more than once, to increase the rate of scutage, the barons were too strong for them. Within little more than two centuries after the Conquest, the declining value of scutage made it no longer worth collecting. The barons' services and rents lapsed. So, in practice, did the incidents of their tenure,[33] which were also a substantial source of revenue to the Crown, though they survived in theory until 1660. Charles I had tried to revive them along with 'ship money', but the parliament of landed gentry insisted on their abolition before accepting the return of his son to the throne. The Statute of Tenures was passed in the first year of Charles II's reign. The head tenants' lands afforded them a revenue on which they were able to live without having to pay or work for it. Their duties, however, had been taken over by central government, and the professionals[34] who were employed to carry them out had to be paid. To pay them, and make up the lost revenue from freeholders, the Crown had to find money from other sources. Various forms of taxation were invented. It had to come out of earnings or savings, and bore more heavily on the poor than on the rich; especially when, as proved to be the case, the rich were able to avoid some of the taxes.[35]

In early societies in Europe, land was regarded as an inheritance belonging to the family. The present possessor could not alienate it (i.e. sell it or lease it) beyond the period of his lifetime and so deprive his future heirs of their expectancy. But, with the development of commerce, inroads were made upon this doctrine. In England, as early as 1290, by the Statute of *Quia Emptores,* inferior tenants were enabled to alienate their land on condition that the purchaser held the land thereafter from the seller's feudal lord on the same terms as the seller had done. When head tenants sold any of their land, this resulted in ever increasing numbers of under-tenants becoming direct tenants of the Crown. Even so, under the Tudors the stability of land tenure was still too strict for the restless, thrusting commercialism of those times. There was land hunger in England, and dabbling in real estate by capitalists

---

33 Listed by Blackstone as aids, relief, primer seisin, wardship, marriage, fines for alienation and escheat.
34 In the Hundred Years War, the feudal chivalry of France were often faced with professional archers who proved too much for them.
35 Before the Revolution in France, the nobility were immune from much of the taxation. In England, from the thirteenth century onwards taxation took the form of a fraction, eventually 'fifteenths and tenths', of the movable wealth of the whole nation, except the very poorest. But the rich had ample opportunities for avoidance. See Kenneth Jupp, *Stealing Our Land*, pp.54-5 and 59.

kept the law courts busy from one end of the country to the other with claims arising out of land.[36]

The Effects of Enclosures and Clearances

ENGLAND IN the sixteenth century was dominated by the question of enclosure: neither the English enclosures nor the later Scottish clearances were given the space they deserved in the standard English history books of later centuries. Only comparatively recently have the effects of Scottish clearances been brought to light by John Prebble, in *The Highland Clearances*.[37] The enclosures in England were a long-drawn-out affair. They had already been going on sporadically for a long time when they were accelerated by the Black Death of 1348-9, and by the Wars of the Roses which followed the Hundred Years War. The early Tudors passed statutes prohibiting enclosure as well as vagrancy laws to punish landless vagabonds. Cardinal Wolsey appointed fifteen commissions to enquire into the result.

> The Inquiry of 1517 showed that in Bedfordshire, Leicestershire and Warwickshire the chances of eviction were about even for tenants on both lay and ecclesiastical estates ... In Leicestershire the enclosure carried out by the Abbey of Leicester (notably Baggrave and Ingardsby) prompted the violent attack of Thomas Rous: 'It is a den of thieves and murderers. The profits of the enclosures the monks enjoy ... but the blood of those slain and mutilated there cries every year to God for vengeance.'[38]

A good share of the responsibility did fall upon the Church. The monastic foundations were possessed of extensive estates, which they administered very efficiently, and in the surge of 'improvement' the ecclesiastical landlords were prominent. But they were by no means the worst offenders. Blame could be allotted to all classes.

Poverty
Government had, however, long ceased to be concerned with the settlement of people on land, and trade in land was followed by the destruction of villages in order to turn land over to sheep and, later, to other

---

36 J.B. Black, *The Reign of Elizabeth*, Oxford University Press, 2nd edn, 1959, p.159.
37 John Prebble, *The Highland Clearances*, London, Secker & Warburg, 1963, 12th reprint 1982 (it achieved twelve reprints in nineteen years).
38 Peter Ramsay, *Tudor Economic Problems*, Gollancz, 1972, pp.27-8.

more profitable purposes. Inevitably, a body of landless paupers, driven out of their homes and villages, deprived of their means of livelihood, began to appear on the highways, endeavouring to support themselves and their families by hook or by crook. 'The beggars had come to town.' By Elizabeth's reign the problem had become explosive.

> The great floating population of vagabonds who used [the roads] presented a problem which could not be ignored. Here the need for action on a nation-wide scale was more than ever apparent, for in spite of all previous attempts to control the plague of beggars their numbers had increased so greatly as to constitute a grave menace to public order ... the 'vagabonds' or 'sturdy beggars' alone numbered 10,000 ... There were no fewer than twenty-three categories of thieves and swindlers ... Such was the composition of this 'merry England' that slept in hay lofts, sheep-cotes, or on doorsteps, spreading terror in the country and disease in the towns.[39]

Pauper enactments in 1563, 1572 and 1601 eventually established the rating system to support the 'impotent, aged and needy'. 'For the rogues it was whipping, and in the last resort if they continued in their roguery, death for felony.' The descendants of the dispossessed, wrenched from their connection with the land and often parted from their families, were sucked into the towns to find work, if they could. Those who succeeded were housed in slums. Within a few generations respectable families were reduced either to working as wage slaves or to having to live by their wits.

Parliamentary Enclosures

In the late eighteenth century parliament completely changed its policy. Enclosure acts under the Tudors had been acts to *prevent* enclosure. Now they had become Acts to *authorise* enclosures, which were turning more and more of the common people out of their villages to make way for 'improvement'. The time from the accession of Queen Anne to 1805 saw the enclosure of 4,187,056 acres.[40] The number of private enclosure bills passed by parliament reached its peak in the reign of George III (1760-1820).

---

39 J.B. Black, *The Reign of Elizabeth*, pp.264-5.
40 The General Report of the Board of Agriculture on Enclosures, cited in J.L. & B. Hammond, *The Village Labourer*, London, Longmans, Green, 1948, Vol. 1, p.35.

The evictions led inevitably to increasing difficulty in maintaining internal peace. Draconian laws to prevent crime were ineffective. Yet the horrors of whipping, prison hulks on the Thames and transportation first to the Americas, later to Botany Bay and Van Diemen's Land, were not connected in the public mind with the victims of enclosure who had no means of making a living except by crowding into urban slums in the hope of scratching a bare subsistence in the appalling conditions of mines, factories and 'service'.[41] The historian G.M. Trevelyan explains:

> But the England of George III was completely aristocratic in the sympathies and constitution of its governing class, whether Whigs, Tories, or 'King's friends' bore rule. The Houses of Parliament which passed the Enclosure Acts were closed by law to anyone who was not a considerable owner of land. The Justices of the Peace were autocrats of the countryside and represented one class alone. The proprietorship of most of the land of England was in the hands of a comparatively small group of 'great noble families'. Under these social and political conditions it was inevitable that the enclosures should be carried through according to the ideas of the big landlord class alone. Those ideas rightly envisaged the national necessity of more food production, but not the national necessity of maintaining and increasing small properties or small holdings.[42]

Capital Punishment

From this time forward capital punishment became more and more common. In 1821 Sir Thomas Buxton told the House of Commons:

> Men there are living today, at whose birth our code contained less than 70 capital offences; and we have seen that number trebled. It is a fact that there stand upon our code 150 offences, made capital during the last century. It is a fact that 600 men were condemned to death last year upon statutes passed within that century. And it is a fact that a great proportion of those who were executed were executed on statutes thus comparatively recent.

Providentially, the great navigators and explorers, from Columbus in the fourteenth century to Captain Cook in the eighteenth, had been discovering new continents to which emigration and the transportation of convicts to penal settlements was possible. These new continents also afforded space for the dispossessed of Europe – particularly, in the

41 Kenneth Jupp, *Stealing Our Land*, pp.25-7.
42 G.M. Trevelyan, *History of England*, p.611.

nineteenth century, for the dispossessed of central Europe. It was clearly providential, for the explorers' own motives were different. Many, for example, thought they were engaged in finding a westward sea route to China, and Columbus is said to have hailed his land-fall in the Caribbean as the entry to paradise.

The death penalty had been mitigated by the alternative of a terrible extension of the Saxon punishments of 'outlawry' and 'abjuring the realm'. The majority of those convicted were pardoned on condition they consent to transportation to America, where labour was in great demand. Following American independence (1776), transportation was switched to Australia, where the Botany Bay expedition arrived in 1787.[43] In the intervening years, according to Burke, 100,000 untransported prisoners were being retained in gaol, or in hulks on the Thames; 558 of them were packed into Newgate prison.

Highland Clearances

A good deal later the same process of land improvement led to the infamous Highland 'clearances'. The clan system had been weakened by the absence of some of the chiefs who had been drawn into the society of the Scottish Stuarts[44] who were now kings of England. In the Highlands of Scotland, their factors adopted a policy of clearing the villages in such a harsh manner that many families were driven to camp on the foreshore to await shipping to the Americas. Kipling's genius in *Captains Courageous* was to describe an American fishing vessel in Newfoundland waters which had on board a Negro cook whose language was Gaelic! His 'folk had run in there in our war' – to Cape Breton in Newfoundland during the American Civil War. He was an escaped slave who had been brought up in a Gaelic speaking Highland family who were victims of the clearances.

---

43   930 had set out; 311 died on the way; 450 were sick; many of the remainder were incurably idle. So said Captain Phillip's report home.
44   The Stuarts were in fact descended from a younger son of a Norman family. He had 'gone North' to seek his fortune.

New Found Lands

THE HISTORY of the settlement of the newly discovered continents shows the mistakes made in the Old World being repeated in the formation of societies in the New World. It has been clearly described by Locke, especially in relation to the settlement of the wide open spaces of Northern America, in which he showed a great interest. He used it as an indicator of how mankind spread throughout the world. 'In the beginning', he said, 'all the world was America.'[45]

In those circumstances, Locke held, nature places a limit on the amount of labour which a man can perform, and a limit on how long the products of the earth last before they decay. These limits restrict men from taking more than a certain amount of land. It seems reasonable, therefore, for anyone to take as much of it as he can make use of to any advantage in life, before its products spoil. It then becomes his property.[46] The laws of nature further restrict the amount of land that a man can enclose because he cannot defend it except by working it; and certainly anyone working it for him will expect to keep the whole of the produce for which he alone will have laboured. Thus the wealth extracted from the earth belonged to the settler by virtue of the labour he had exerted in obtaining it, and the land he enclosed for the purpose was his by the right of labour: 'as much land as a man tills, plants, improves, cultivates, and can use the product of, so much is his property'. The appropriation of land was not 'any prejudice to any other man, since there was still enough and as good left'.[47]

However, as Locke observed, the invention of money overcame the constraints imposed by nature upon taking more land than a man and his family could personally manage. The excess production, which formerly had to be used quickly or else left to rot, could now be exchanged for coins, which were virtually imperishable, and the hoarding of which could make men rich.

As the settlers in the new found lands grew in number, they formed small societies, hamlets and villages, which gradually enlarged into

---

45 He meant, of course, that there had originally been plenty of unappropriated land available in the Old World.
46 John Locke, *Second Treatise of Government*, paragraph 31.
47 *Ibid.* paragraphs 32-3.

towns. It was a natural step to set up a government to which all but a few willingly submitted, and those few were forced to submit. One of the first actions of this government was to pass laws to protect the convention that land enclosed by the first settlers belonged to them, or to any later conquerors, and continued to be their property even though they no longer worked that land.[48] Thus property in land in the New World came to be protected by the same human convention and law as prevailed in the Old World. The basis of such rough justice is no more substantial than the popular saying 'finders keepers' or the maxim 'might is right', but it results in nature being unable any longer to keep land free.

A-R.J. Turgot (1727-81), extending Locke's conception, pointed out that a nation's territory never has been, nor ever can be, equally divided among its inhabitants. The capabilities of individuals differ, and parcels of land differ in fertility and other advantages. This makes equal division impossible. Moreover, as land is passed on to the next and subsequent generations, it is cut into larger or smaller portions according to the number of inheritors to be provided for, and inequality is thereby increased. This was perfectly understood in Old Testament times, and was provided against in the Torah, which enjoined the re-allotment of land in every jubilee year.[49] This is an example of divine law revealed in scripture which has been largely ignored, not least by the Church, and in consequence by subsequent governments of every complexion.

This difference both in land and in people nevertheless had its advantages, which in themselves could be regarded as providential. It compelled individual men or families to concentrate on producing what suited their own land best, and to trade whatever they produced beyond their own requirements with the production of others, obtaining in return the things they could not or did not produce themselves. The benefit of this specialisation is that it increases production overall, while trading ensures that excess production is consumed and nothing is wasted.

As already observed, a nation's territory is no less variegated than the people who inhabit it. The soil may be fertile or barren; a stretch of land may be suited only to particular products; some land may even be

---

48 A-R.J. Turgot, *Réfléxions*. See Kenneth Jupp's translation, *The Formation and Distribution of Wealth*, London, Othila Press, 1999, paragraphs 9, 17.

49 See especially Leviticus 25. Many of the prophets refer to its frequent neglect, with disastrous results in terms of poverty, and slavery to redeem debts. Christ repeated the theme in the New Testament, especially in Luke 4:16ff, after which the people of his home town attempted to assassinate him.

useless in the existing state of knowledge. The first settlers naturally occupy what seems to be the best land – as much as, or more than, their talents and the size of their families can manage. Those who come later have to content themselves with second and then with third best, and so on until the time comes when all workable land is taken up, and, as Turgot puts it, 'every land has an owner'. At the margin of society there remains a great deal of land which is too poor to provide a livelihood.

Employment

WHEN 'EVERY land has an owner', newcomers have no choice but to seek employment by a landowner, or to set up in business in secondary industry which processes the raw products of the earth so as to make them suitable for human consumption. Grain is made into flour, and then into bread, hides into leather and leather goods, timber into wood, and then into all manner of wooden objects. Secondary industry such as that of millers, farmers and blacksmiths can relieve the agriculturist of some of the work that is more efficiently done by specialists.

If settlement continues, newcomers begin to compete with each other for work, and naturally the employer bargains with the worker over the wage he is to pay, in the same way as he bargains with his shoemaker over the price of his shoes. In each case he buys the least expensive. Competition soon reduces wages to subsistence level.[50]

Secondary Workers
For these secondary occupations the worker has to have space in the nation's territory for his house, together with his mill, smithy, bakery or workshop, and it will need to be within easy reach of the agriculturists who are his customers. Land of that sort will already have been enclosed; it will be protected by law and convention. With every piece of land having an owner, rent will have to be paid to him for permission to set up business there. The secondary worker, unlike the earlier settlers, is no longer independent, he is subject to a landlord. As payment for his permission for his land to be used, the landlord takes the surplus arising from the superior position of the land.

---

50 The foregoing three paragraphs are based on Turgot's *Réfléxions*, paragraphs 1-15, where these observations are beautifully set out. See Kenneth Jupp's translation, *The Formation and Distribution of Wealth*.

Millionaires

One unavoidable result of the convention and law described above is the emergence in new found lands of a crop of millionaires. It was a feature of the opening up of America to Western culture during the last two centuries. Population increased by leaps and bounds. People who had enclosed open land when a territory was uninhabited eventually found themselves, sometimes in a remarkably short time, at the centre of a densely populated town or city, where land is rented or sold by the square foot. Others found themselves to be the owners of land rich in minerals, particularly oil, which were much in demand after advances in science and technology had discovered important uses for them. The same convention and law made it impossible to exploit these resources without the owner's permission; and for that he could charge royalties. He could become 'Mr Five per cent'.[51] Very often the Old World benefited from the wealth of these millionaires: there are charitable trusts in England today which are still distributing their benevolence to the needy.

Similar enrichment in Australia is graphically illustrated by Dickens's character Magwitch in *Great Expectations.* Today we see the same growth of millionaires in Russia as its lands (rich in every kind of natural wealth), the property of government since the Communist regime, are still being allotted (as they used to be then) to individuals and syndicates without the government charging them a proper rent. They become a 'Mafia', who themselves charge rent enough to those they allow to use the land. The latter remain poor. The former are very rich.

Ricardo's Law of Rent

BECAUSE OF the inequality of lands, if the first-comers have the best land they will, with equal skill, effort and capital expenditure, inevitably produce more than those who have to be content with second-best land. The latter will nevertheless be able to produce more than those with third-grade land, and so on. The result is that those on the best land produce each year a revenue which reflects the superiority of their position. This is greater than the revenue produced on second-grade

51 The nickname of the Azerbaijani oil millionaire Gulbenkian.

land, greater still than that produced on lower grades of land. There is thus an ever-increasing surplus in comparison with lower grades of land until at 'the margin' the quality of available land is such that it will not afford a living, much less produce a surplus.[52] Land beyond the margin is 'waste' or 'desert', although that does not necessarily mean that it will be without an owner.

This 'law of rent' is true not only of agricultural land but also of land on which a workshop, office, shop etc is built. On land at the heart of that part of society which makes use of them, the goods or services produced there will be more profitable than on land further out. At the margin a point will come where there are not enough clients or customers to make it worth trying to get a living there. Where the margin lies is different for every occupation. In every kind of productive activity – farming, industry, trading, commerce or professional services – there is a varying degree of surplus of this nature, from the centre down the scale to its margin.

By convention and man-made law this surplus has always belonged to the landowner. The result, when those who owned the land they worked on, was that those with a surplus could either work less hard for the same return or, by continuing to work hard, amass far greater riches

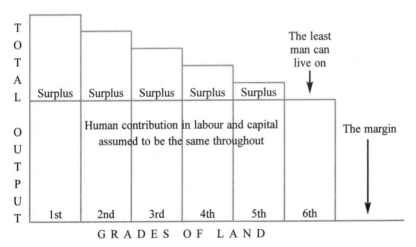

52 See Ricardo, *The Principles of Politics and Taxation*, London, Everyman, 1962, Chapter 2, especially p.35.

than could those less fortunately placed.[53] However, when the surplus
grows large enough, it is only to be expected that some should find ways
of having others work their land for them while they themselves live on
the revenue they receive, and enjoy a life of leisure. In the competitive
conditions of employment, wages are reduced to subsistence level and,
after the capitalist takes his interest, and the entrepreneur his profit, the
surplus beyond that is the revenue due to the landowner. Ricardo's law
is described in the simple diagram on page 39.

Duties of Government

THAT MAN cannot live except on the dry surface of the earth, and cannot get a living except from the earth's resources, is a matter of evident
sense. It is therefore equally evident that these resources must somehow
be shared. This is affirmed both by natural law as discovered by reason
and by divine law as revealed in Scripture. John Locke cited both as
authority for the necessity to share the earth's bounty:

> Whether we consider natural reason, which tells us that men being once born
> have a right to their preservation, and consequently to meat and drink and
> such other things as nature affords for their subsistence; or Revelation, which
> gives us an account of those grants God made of the world to Adam, and to
> Noah, and his sons; it is very clear, that God, as King David says, Psalm cxv
> 16, has given the earth to the children of men; given it in common.[54]

Thus the first duty of government arises from the essential requirement that every family unit of a nation has to have a home and a means
of livelihood. Any family which lacks these things must either perish or
be an incubus on the rest of society, supported by charity, as in former
times, or, as in modern times, by poor relief (now called 'welfare' but
fast becoming 'ill-fare') provided by the state and funded by the taxpayer. The other essential duties of government are defence of the realm
and maintenance of internal peace. In the earliest forms of society this
first duty was no problem because all families were provided with land.

---

53 All newly settled territories inevitably in time produce a crop of millionaires. Fortunately, Christian charity influences many of them to set up trusts and foundations to dispose of their surpluses in good works
of education, healing the sick and relieving poverty.
54 John Locke, *Second Treatise of Government*, paragraph 25. There are, of course a number of other scriptural references to the subject in both Old and New Testaments, although they are not much in evidence
in the teaching of the modern Church.

In the modern world a fundamental cause of injustice arises from the neglect by governments of all descriptions of this first duty. All over the world there is poverty, homelessness and, in the worst areas, famine, while taxpayers in some countries are obliged to pay subsidies to have fertile ground set aside, so that it does not produce too much, and abundant materials do not remain unsold.

Through the Looking Glass

COMPARING THE LOT of the employed man of today with the condition of his Saxon forebears reveals that, surprisingly perhaps, little has changed.

In the USA, the paragon of 'capitalism' in our enlightened times, 'Tax Freedom Day' falls early in June. This date is calculated by imagining that all the employees' taxes at all levels are concentrated at the beginning of the year rather than being spread throughout the year. On this basis the average American could begin working for himself instead of for the government after this date.[55] In Great Britain, the equivalent 'Tax Independence Day' has been declared to be 15 June. While conditions in Saxon England and under feudalism were not uniform, taken as a whole the number of days a year the average peasant was obligated to labour on his lord's demesne was no greater than the 128 an average American today is obliged to work for Uncle Sam. It was certainly less than the 137 days that most of the Queen's subjects in Britain now work for the exchequer. There were cases where certain groups of peasants had to work 147 days a year or even longer. However, for his labour, the medieval peasant received protection and, in addition, a cottage and field, and access to the village commons. His lord, without payment, would have set him up for life with livestock, implements of husbandry and necessary household furnishings. On top of his labour, some *geboras* paid ten pence to their lord at Michaelmas, and 23 bushels of barley and two hens at Easter.

In Saxon times the *gebur* was the lowest class of tenant farmer. His precise position is something of a mystery. He seems to have held a *yardland* (a quarter of a *hide*?) which was the typical villein tenement of

---

55 Calculation by the US Tax Foundation, Washington, DC.

the middle ages. Its acreage would vary, as did the acreage of the hide, in different districts, but 30 acres would be a reasonable guess at the average size of a yardland. For this he had to perform a heavy burden of services, and pay some money and some rents in kind. Sir Frank Stenton lists these, as extracted from the *Rectitudines*:[56] his ordinary service would require him to work for his lord two days each week of the year, three at harvest and between Candlemas (2 February) and Easter. He was in addition required to plough an acre a week from the start of the autumn ploughing after harvest until Martinmas (11 November). As 'boon work', during which he was fed – sometimes sumptuously – he was expected on request to plough three acres a year. In return for his pasture rights he ploughed two acres a year, and as rent for his holding a further three acres, providing his lord with the necessary seed corn for these three acres. In the winter from Martinmas to Easter he took his turn as watchman at his lord's fold. He paid ten pence to his lord at Michaelmas; 23 bushels of barley and two hens at Martinmas; and either a young sheep or two pence at Easter.

That advances in science and technology over more than a thousand years should have produced no greater freedom for labour requires investigation. Why are we so little better off? Are we indeed better off at all? Direct comparison is impossible, and some of the suppositions in the foregoing paragraph may be doubtful. But one thing is beyond doubt. By however much science and technology have increased the productivity of a man's labour, only a very small proportion of the benefit of it has accrued to the labourer.

As Alice remarked:

'Everything is just as it was!'
'Of course it is,' said the Queen 'what else would you have it?'
'Well in our country,' said Alice, still panting a little, 'you'd generally get to somewhere else if you ran very fast for a long time, as we've been doing.'

---

56 *Rectitudines Singularum Personarum*, cited in F.M. Stenton, *Anglo-Saxon England*, pp.473-6, which dates it from the generation before the Conquest.

3

The Rule of Law

T ODAY IT IS widely accepted that there can be no justice without the rule of law. But what does 'the rule of law' mean? On the face of it, it would appear to be a peculiarly English notion, but this is misleading. Certainly the US and Canada inherited the concept from the Old World, chiefly through the works of Locke and Blackstone, on which the Founding Fathers of the United States based their deliberations when drafting the Declaration of Independence. In 1981 Canada's Constitution Act boldly stated that 'Canada is founded upon principles that recognise the *Supremacy of God* and the *Rule of Law*'. In 1990, President Bush (senior) explained to Congress that one of the objectives of the Gulf War was 'a New World Order in which *the rule of law* supplants the law of the jungle'. In 1999 Prime Minister Blair, on a visit to the United States, justified the war against Serbia by suggesting it was in our national interest to 'establish the values of liberty, *the rule of law,* human rights, and an open society'.[57] What law is it, of which they were so anxious to establish the rule? It cannot have been Iraqi law, or Serbian law, or any local law: the assassination of Saddam Hussein, or of Slobodan Milosevic, contrary to those laws, would have been welcomed. The attempted assassination of Hitler half a century ago would have been equally welcomed, had it succeeded.

The Declaration of Independence

WITHOUT A FULL understanding of what is meant by 'the rule of law', this rhetoric is so much hot air. This was apparent when the American founding fathers, although inspired by the philosophy of Locke and

---

57 *Daily Telegraph,* 23 April 1999 (St George's Day), pp.1-2.

Blackstone, nevertheless turned a blind eye to Blackstone's condemnation of slavery.[58] They ignored Locke's insistence on the freedom of the person, his right to all his handiwork, and the divine injunction to hold land in common for all mankind.[59] All the founding fathers were extensive landowners; many had slaves. Thomas Jefferson, by whom the Declaration was chiefly drafted, had children by a slave mistress. He owned 105 slaves on his land (over 5,500 acres) in Albermarle County, and a further 49 slaves on his lands in Bedford County. He did at times sell slaves to pay his creditors (even so he died in debt to the extent of $100,000).[60] In theory Jefferson had long been opposed to slavery and had suggested various ways of abolishing it, but he was unable to persuade his colleagues. The outcome was that the famous Declaration of 4 July 1776 stated only:

> that all men are created equal, that they are endowed by their creator with certain inalienable rights, that among these are Life, Liberty, and the pursuit of Happiness – that to secure these rights, Governments are instituted among men …

There was no reference to the right of ownership of the work of one's own hands or to freedom of the person for slaves. One can only be wryly amused at the idea of a landless slave's liberty and pursuit of happiness. In fact it took a further half century, and a bloody civil war, to abolish slavery. Moreover, at the end of it, the landless black, without an owner to take care of him as part of his property, was often a good deal worse off than when he was a slave. After emancipation, when too old to work he could be, and often was, left to starve. Even today the distinction between the landed and the landless remains as evident in the US as anywhere in the world.

---

58 Blackstone, *Commentaries*, Vol. 1, pp.123 and 412. See facsimile of the 1st edn (1765-9), published in 4 volumes in 1979 by the Chicago University Press. In later editions (e.g. the seventh edition of 1775) the first of these references became altered by the deletion of the words 'and with regard to all natural rights becomes *eo instanti* a freeman', and the substitution of the words 'and so far becomes a freeman; though the master's rights to his service may possibly still continue'. The second reference remains unaltered.

59 John Locke, *Second Treatise of Government*, paragraphs 25-6.

60 Noble E. Cunningham, *In Pursuit of Reason: The Life of Thomas Jefferson*, Louisiana State University Press, 1987, p.196.

The Rule of Law in England

THE BEST-KNOWN exposition of the rule of law as a legal principle of the English Constitution was made in 1885 by Professor Dicey in his book *An Introduction to the Law of the Constitution*. He pointed out that, as a characteristic of the English constitution, we generally include under the one expression at least three distinct though kindred conceptions:

> We mean, in the first place, that no man is punishable or can be lawfully made to suffer in body or goods except for a distinct breach of law established in the ordinary legal manner before the ordinary Courts of the land.
>
> We mean in the second place ... that here every man, whatever be his rank or condition, is subject to the ordinary law of the realm and amenable to the jurisdiction of the ordinary tribunals.
>
> [Thirdly] ... the general principles of the constitution (as for example the right to personal liberty, or the right of public meeting) are with us the result of judicial decisions determining the rights of private persons in particular cases brought before the Courts; whereas under many foreign constitutions the security (such as it is) given to the rights of individuals results or appears to result, from the general principles of the constitution.

Earlier Statements of the Rule

IN TRUTH the notion of the rule of law is of ancient origin and meant far more than Dicey allowed. The editor of the modern edition of his book remarked:

> Let no-one suppose that Dicey invented the rule of law. He did, of course, put his own interpretation upon the meaning of that rule. The rule itself, as Holdsworth has shown, may be traced back to the mediaeval notion that law, whether it be attributed to a supernatural or human source, ought to rule the world.[61]

This 'mediaeval notion' of natural law had been propounded for Roman Catholic Europe seven centuries earlier in the *Summa Theologica* of St Thomas Aquinas (1225-74).[62] Above man-made law Aquinas defined: (1) the eternal law – a divine providence to which all things are subject and by which all things are ruled and measured, and

---

61 Professor C.C.S. Wade in the introduction to the 10th edn of Dicey's book, *Introduction to the Study of the Law of the Constitution*, London, Macmillan, 1959, pp.xl and xcvii, where a full note is given of the references in Sir William Holdsworth's voluminous *History of English Law*.
62 *Thomas Aquinas: Selected Writings*, London, Everyman, 1939, pp.81-6.

(2) natural law – which is not something different from the eternal law, but is a participation thereof. 'The light of natural reason, whereby we discern what is good and what is evil, which is the function of the natural law, is nothing else than an imprint on us of the divine light'. The full text is:

> Law, being a rule and measure, can be in a person in two ways: in one way, as in him who rules and measures; in another way, as in that which is ruled and measured, since a thing is ruled and measured in so far as it partakes of the rule and measure. Wherefore, since all things subject to divine providence are ruled and measured by the eternal law, as stated above, it is evident that all things partake somewhat of the eternal law, in so far as, namely, from its being implanted in them, they derive their respective inclinations to their proper acts and ends. Now among all others, the rational creature is subject to divine providence in the most excellent way, in so far as it partakes of a share of providence, by being provident both for itself and others. Wherefore it has a share of the eternal reason, whereby it has a natural inclination to its proper act and end: and this participation of the eternal law in the rational creature is called the natural law ... the light of natural reason, whereby we discern what is good and what is evil, which is the function of the natural law, is nothing else but an imprint on us of the divine light. It is therefore evident that the natural law is nothing else than the rational creature's participation of the eternal law.

In fact the idea of the rule of law can be traced back to classical antiquity and beyond. But we need go no further back than to the eighteenth century when Blackstone, who had a profound influence on the study of law in England, and even more influence in North America, expressed the idea in terms referring specifically to its supernatural source. His view is therefore not very different from that of Aquinas.

Blackstone's *Commentaries*

Blackstone (1723-80) defines law as a rule of action which is prescribed by some superior and which the inferior is bound to obey. He distinguishes between the law of nature and natural law as follows:[63]

> Thus when the supreme being formed the universe, and created matter out of nothing, he impressed certain principles upon that matter, from which it can never depart, and without which it would cease to be, [just as does a workman] when he forms a clock ...

---

63 Blackstone, *Commentaries*, under 'Of the Nature of Laws in General', abridged from pp.38-43 of Vol. 1 of the 1st edn.

[Like the clock] Man, considered as a creature, must necessarily be subject to the laws of his creator, for he is a dependent being ... And consequently, as man depends absolutely upon his creator for every thing, it is necessary he should at all points conform to his maker's will.

This will of his maker is called the law of nature. For as God, when he created matter, and endued it with a principle of mobility, established certain rules for the perpetual direction of that motion; so, when he created man, and endued him with freewill to conduct himself in all parts of his life, he laid down certain immutable laws of human nature, whereby that freewill is in some degree regulated and restrained, and gave him also the faculty of reason to discover the purport of those laws.

But [in his infinite wisdom] he has laid down only such laws as were founded in those relations of justice, that existed in the nature of things antecedent to any positive precept. These are the eternal, immutable laws of good and evil, to which the creator himself in all his dispositions conforms; and which he has enabled human reason to discover, so far as they are necessary for the conduct of human actions. Such among others are ... that we should live honestly; should hurt nobody; and should render to everyone its due; to which three general precepts Justinian has reduced the whole doctrine of the law ...

This is the foundation of what we call ethics, or natural law ... But to apply this to the particular exigencies of each individual, it is necessary to have recourse to reason ... But every man now [i.e. since the fall of Adam] finds that his reason is corrupt, and his understanding full of ignorance and error.

This has given manifold occasion for the benign interposition of divine providence ... to discover and enforce its laws by an immediate and direct revelation. The doctrines thus delivered we call the revealed or divine law, and they are to be found only in holy scriptures. These precepts, when revealed, are found to be really a part of the original law of nature. Yet undoubtedly the revealed law is (humanly speaking) of infinitely more authority than what we generally call the natural law. Because one is the law of nature expressly declared so by God himself; the other is only what, by the assistance of human reason, we imagine to be that law ...

Upon these two foundations, the law of nature and the law of revelation, depend all human laws; that is to say, no human laws should be suffered to contradict these.[64]

The law of nature according to Blackstone consists of such laws as were founded in those relations of justice that existed in the nature of things antecedent to any positive precept, namely the eternal, immutable laws of good and evil to which the Creator himself conforms. They

---

64 Abridged but in his own words, except where enclosed in square brackets.

include among others the three general precepts to which Justinian has reduced the whole doctrine of the law. The point which is noteworthy is that man must conform to the justice to which the Creator himself conforms: he has been given reason by which he may discover what this is, but because his reason is corrupted divine law, as revealed in scripture, is more reliable than what his corrupted reason can discover.

Most ordinary people have a glimmer of understanding (through what they would probably call common sense) that laws ought to conform with justice. It enables them to appreciate Mr Bumble's much-quoted complaint in Dickens's *Oliver Twist*, that 'the law is a ass'. Bumble, the very model of a hen-pecked husband, had just been told that the law assumes your wife acts under your direction! 'If the law says that', he retorted, 'then the law is a ass – an idiot.' We may assume that he had in mind the difference between law and justice. Mankind has never ceased to want some better or higher law, a law which would cover any set of facts and would therefore never be at odds with justice. Every man of common sense carries the idea of natural law in his heart – 'a law above the law'.[65] We may call this simply *justice*, but we should remember it as the law to which the Creator himself conforms.[66] St Paul described the present situation accurately when he said of the Gentiles, 'who have not the law ... these show the law written in their hearts, their conscience also bearing witness, and their thoughts the meanwhile accusing or else excusing one another'.[67]

Evident to Sense

This innate feeling for natural law comes from the fact, which it is almost impossible to overlook, that the whole of the natural world works according to a pre-set plan or system. The times and tides – sunrise, sunset, moonrise, moonset, high water at London Bridge, are there to be read in the newspaper every day. The equinoxes and solstices are noted on the calendar in advance of their happening. Great excitement often occurs

---

65 The title of a book by professor and Lutheran pastor John Warwick Montgomery, Minneapolis, Bethany Fellowship, 1975.

66 In the New Testament, 'justice' is the proper translation of the Greek δικαιοσυνη (√ δικη = decree). In the Authorised Version it is usually translated as 'righteousness', which gives it an unnecessary and misleading religious flavour. With its modern connotation that word aptly describes the Pharisees, who were so righteous that they tithed mint and rue and all manner of herbs but, as Christ warned them, passed over judgement and the love of God (Luke 11:42).

67 Romans 3:14-15.

when the approach of an eclipse of sun is announced. These, and the law of gravity on which many of them depend, have been discovered by man, but the laws have not been changed by being discovered.

There is beauty in the order of the natural universe. Surely it must be possible for man to display the same beauty? Surely it must be natural for mankind to exhibit the same order? And not only mankind as a whole, but individual human beings, and families gathered together in a nation?

Unfortunately, however, when scientists and technicians in the eighteenth century devised rams to make water run uphill, in the nineteenth century made trains, and later motor cars, to run at unbelievable speeds, and in the twentieth century produced aeroplanes to defy gravity by carrying tons of freight into the skies, mankind's belief in the need for divine providence was replaced by the belief that man can fashion the universe for his own ends. 'I am the master of my soul', he says, 'I am the captain of my fate'. Herein lies the illusion of mankind as he ignores his dependence on the divine providence of the Creator (and notwithstanding the many different names He has been given by different religions through the ages).

The French Revolution

1789 and its sequel, more than anything else, shattered religious faith. The sheer violence and futility of the Terror which caused the death of 40,000 Frenchmen, 17,000 of them under the guillotine,[68] shocked the Western world. English radicals at first welcomed the Revolution but, following the Terror, many gradually defected to Pitt and there followed a suppression of radical thought, with courts in England and Scotland in 1792-3 sentencing the secretary of the Corresponding Society to prison and the secretary of the Scottish Friends of the People, a leading Scottish Unitarian and ex-fellow of a Cambridge college, to transportation. In 1794 habeas corpus was suspended. The strain of the Napoleonic Wars made matters worse. In 1798 newspapers were put under the supervision of the magistrates, and in the following year many reforming societies were suppressed. Persecution of the Church in Continental Europe in the nineteenth century caused many religious people to emigrate to Britain

---

68 The figure given by the French historian Henri Taine. Some say it should be considerably higher.

and America.[69] The idea of natural law withered throughout the century. In the Church, Traditionalism denied that natural law can be known by unaided human reason, while Rationalism denied its dependence on God as the author of nature. Its very existence is denied by many modern philosophers.[70]

Lawyers Reject Natural Law

Writing in 1966, Professor Keeton described the effect of this on the English legal system:

> For nearly a century, Christian usages and Christian doctrine have been steadily legislated out of English law. As the late Richard O'Sullivan pointed out, the Common Law had owed many of its noblest concepts to Christian theology. The soul of man was acknowledged to have an individual relation with God, which transcended the claims of society, and, in consequence, jurisprudence was founded upon moral principles directly derived from Christian theology. From this there emerged the concept of equality of all men as bearers of rights and duties before the law, exactly as they were equal in the sight of God.[71]

But in fact the laws of nature remained inviolate, inexorable, unconquered and unconquerable. It was merely that the scientists and technicians had discovered a great deal about a very specific sub-set of natural laws, namely those seen in the physical sciences, and could make use of those newly discovered laws to accomplish what, to the uninstructed, looked like miracles. Learn from the birds: give the vehicle wings, design the shape of the wings in such a way that the wind presses more powerfully from below than it does above the wing, make the vehicle go fast enough to create a strong current of air – and, hey presto! The vehicle rises in the air. That is a crude, probably inaccurate, summary of what happened, but it does indicate how the laws of nature have been used and obeyed. They have not been altered one jot. Newton's own assessment of his discoveries, so well known that it requires an apology for quoting it, expresses a more appropriate attitude:

---

69 Quarr Abbey was founded at the beginning of this century in the Isle of Wight as a refuge where the exiles from Solesmes could preserve their Gregorian chant.
70 *Oxford Dictionary of the Christian Church*, 1958 edn, under 'Natural Law'. A more recent edition declares that modern philosophers have for the most part abandoned the theory.
71 G.W. Keeton, *The Norman Conquest and the Common Law*, 1966.

I don't know what I may seem to the world, but as to myself, I seem to have been only like a boy playing on the sea-shore and diverting myself in finding a smoother pebble or a prettier shell than ordinary, whilst the great ocean of truth lay all undiscovered before me.[72]

The humility displayed by Newton was lacking in most of the philosophers, economists, historians, politicians and lawyers who had not understood Blackstone. They turned from natural law, whether discovered by reason or revelation, and adopted the Machiavellian view that law is 'what the all-powerful Prince (i.e. the government) wills'. By the end of the nineteenth century Europe was ready to embark on an adventure of socialism which would invade the lives of all sorts and conditions of men, regulating them in whatever way governments judged best. This came to be called 'the command or *dirigiste* economy'. The public were deceived. The result in all the countries that took wholeheartedly to socialism after the First World War was to inflate the ego of the rulers and to beat the common people into subjection. After the Second World War a movement started which preferred bureaucratic government to the corrupt government of individual sovereign nations. In establishing the European Union the public were deceived again, although realisation seems now to be dawning that this may have been jumping out of the frying pan into the fire.

De Tocqueville
The French historian Alexis de Tocqueville (1805-69), born like Turgot of an ancient Norman family, achieved fame in Europe and America in his lifetime as a liberal whose views challenged both the overthrow of the old order and the extremism of the Republicans. He condemned the authoritarian government of the Revolution, continued and intensified by Napoleon and the Bourbon monarchs who followed him, and thereafter by the Emperor Louis Napoleon in the Second Empire of 1851. De Tocqueville's consistent theme was the mistake made in attempting to introduce reforms by means of despotic government, whether royal, aristocratic or popular. 'The French sought reform before seeking liberty.' He compared France unfavourably with England and America, where the primary concern was to establish liberty.

---

72 J. Osborn (ed), Joseph Spence, *Observations, Anecdotes ...*, Oxford, Clarendon Press, 1996, No. 1295.

De Tocqueville enjoyed popular acclaim for his analysis twice during his lifetime, but his work was forgotten later in the nineteenth century. After the two world wars of the twentieth century, the upsurge of total-itarian governments revived public interest in de Tocqueville. He was appealed to as a prophet of liberal political philosophy who believed that class distinction would disappear only if authoritarian governments of all kinds were curtailed. His view was the direct opposite of that of Karl Marx, who urged the adoption of totalitarian governments to wage class warfare on the privileged.

Government and the Rule of Law

A SOVEREIGN government of whatever form has the power to make any laws it pleases to bind all its subjects, but governments which recognise the rule of law, as described by Aquinas and Blackstone, would ensure that their laws were in harmony with nature. This would involve endeavouring to conform not only to the laws discovered by the natural sciences, but also to natural law, whether discovered by reason or revealed in scripture, which restrains the free will of human kind.

Unfortunately, throughout the nineteenth and twentieth centuries antagonism between science and religion developed to such an extent that today there is a distinct split between them. Few scientists have regard to scripture and few theologians connect the scriptures with science. In truth, of course, both science and religion are concerned with the laws which govern the whole universe. It may well be that each could profit from seeking the help of the other.

Religion Today
Religion today appears to be a very divisive force, setting nation against nation even to the point of war. Muslim 'fundamentalists' are set against both Jews and Christians. Christians still persecute Jews in a number of countries. In Israel, Jews kill Palestinian Muslims and vice versa. This is, however, only religion on the surface. None of the three religions actually gives authority for such actions. This is nothing new. Judaism, Christianity and Islam have each been disgraced in similar fashion at various times in their history. Witness, for example, the

crucifixion of Jesus, the slaughter of the Quraiza Jews at Medina (27), and the Crusaders' notorious sack of Jerusalem (1099).

In January 2002 Pope John Paul II, at the third of the inter-religious meetings he organised, addressed representatives of the world religions at Assisi on the subject of peace. He urged them 'to repudiate the violence that seeks to clothe itself in religion, appealing even to the most holy name of God'. His Holiness laid stress on:

> the two pillars upon which peace rests: commitment to justice and readiness to forgive. Justice, first of all, because there can be no true peace without respect for the dignity of persons and peoples, respect for the rights and duties of each person and respect for an equal distribution of benefits and burdens between individuals and in society as a whole. It can never be forgotten that situations of oppression and exclusion are often the source of violence and terrorism. But forgiveness too, because… forgiveness alone heals the wounds of the heart and fully restores damaged human relations.

The world's various religions, and the branches or sects into which they are sub-divided, have a common core of essential creed. But in the course of time this essential core has been enhanced by myth or disfigured by differences of language and emphasis, by historical anomalies or by organisational necessities, until ultimately the basic core is not easily recognised.

In Judaism the ten commandments in the Old Covenant are an outstanding example of this essential core. In the New Covenant the summary of the law given by Jesus to the lawyer who tempted him (Matthew 22:39), 'Love thy neighbour as thyself,' is even more remarkable because it is so comprehensive in spite of its incisive brevity. The Lord's Prayer, which Jesus taught his disciples when they asked him how they should to pray,[73] has been said to contain the whole Christian doctrine.

The Lord's Prayer

The prayer is addressed to the transcendent God 'in heaven': One and only One. It ends with a threefold doxology which reminds us of the succeeding ages during which the immanent God rules, empowers and beautifies the universe. In between there are seven suffrages, in groups of three. The first three, directed heavenward, concern our relationship with God, the last three our relationship with other people. In between

---

73 The Lord's Prayer, Luke 11:2-4

these two triads, the fourth petition makes the connection between earth and heaven. Thus the prayer embraces in graceful variety the numbers one, three and seven:

> Our Father which art in heaven
> 1   Hallowed be Thy Name
> 2   Thy Kingdom come
> 3   Thy Will be done
> 4   As in Heaven, so on earth, Give us this day our daily bread[74]
> 5   And forgive us our failings as we forgive them that fail us
> 6   And lead us not into temptation
> 7   But deliver us from evil.
>   For Thine is the Kingdom, the Power, and the Glory, for ever…
>   and ever…

In the first triad, we are to revere the Holy Name,[75] to accept the divine rule and to bow to the divine will. In the final triad we seek forgiveness to the extent that we forgive others; we ask not to be tempted but we beg for rescue when we fall. The middle petition connects the other two parts: 'As in Heaven, so on earth'.[76] It asks that we be fed each day with food for body, mind and spirit.[77] Together with the other two parts it forms yet another trinity.

Hinduism

The nearest equivalent to what might be described as a national or official religion amongst the Hindus of India has from very early times been the *A-dwa-ita* tradition. Its title translates literally as 'a-two-ity', but is usually referred to as *non-dualism*. It describes the tradition inaugurated by the philosopher and teacher Shankara at some time between the fifth and third centuries BC.[78] Its holy books are the Vedas, the Upanishads and the Bhagavadgita. Somehow it seems to have escaped notice that *A-dwa-ita* is strictly both monotheistic and trinitarian. The transcendent God is

---

74 There is no punctuation in the manuscripts prior to the ninth century. The translation here made fits the Greek precisely.

75 Exodus 3:14.

76 ως εν τοις ουρανοις και επι της γης. The English translations usually reverse the order and the meaning.

77 'The spiritual food of the most blessed body and blood', the Holy Spirit to direct and rule our hearts. St Jerome translated 'daily bread' as '*panem superstantialem*', and this was how it was rendered in Latin Bibles.

78 This date is subject to much dispute today. See 'Shankarâchâria, date of' in Ernest Wood's *Vedânta Dictionary,* Philosophical Library, New York, 1963.

the *Param Âtman* (the Supreme Self, the *I am* of the universe), and 'the creation is full of 'the three *Gunas* ("strands" as in a rope), which repeat right through creation from the very first impulse to the very end'.[79]

This Hindu tradition describes the essential core, referred to above, as *Sanâtana Dharma*, the everlasting way (in the sense of way of life) or the everlasting law.

> The *Sanâtana Dharma* is the original, the root of all religions, and of the religions we see today. It is not necessary to embrace *Sanâtana Dharma*. Every religion contains it. If each one follows his own religion truthfully, he would for certain be following *Sanâtana Dharma*. It is the basis of all religions and their centre. There is no need to change anybody's present religion.[80]

This surely is the root of the rule of law: the governance in the hearts and minds of men and women of that body of principle which makes up the natural way of living, drawn from natural law and expressing our common humanity. Far from being merely a legal principle or concept, the rule of law lies at the heart of what it is to be human and is a principle of daily conduct, 'to act lawfully'. The rule of law is not the rule of any old law. Under this natural rule of law everyone is my neighbour and, if judgement must be meted out, care is taken to ensure the law is followed and judgement and enforcement are meted out by independent, impartial, competent judges so that equilibrium is restored and justice may be found. As Plato says, as in the individual, so in the state. Under such a rule of law the horrors of recent ethnic cleansing would be unthinkable.

---

79 So described by HH the Shankârâcharia of North India in *Good Company*, Shaftesbury, Dorset, Element Books, 1992, p.72.
80 *Ibid.* p.125.

4

Philosophy, Science and Religion

*From the intrinsic evidence of his creation, the Great Architect of the
Universe now begins to appear as a pure mathematician.*[81]

Music and Mathematics

IN WRITING this in 1930, Sir James Jeans, astronomer, physicist and
mathematician, had behind him a tradition stretching back to at least
the fifth century BC. It appears especially in Plato's dialogue
Timaeus, in Aristotle's description of the Pythagorean doctrine, and the
fragments of Greek authors describing the work, as they supposed, of
Pythagoras himself, whose system has sometimes been said to be
founded on the belief that 'God is a mathematician'. Aristotle himself
remarked on the 'threeness of things'. According to him, the Pythagoreans said, 'Things are number,' and 'Things imitate number.'[82] Newton
too, in the beginning of his *Philosophiae Naturalis Principia,* described
his purpose as: '*Missis formis substantialibus et qualitatibus occultis
phenomina naturae ad leges mathematicas revocare*' ('to apply the
mathematical laws to the phenomena of nature in their manifest forms
and hidden qualities').

Independently of this tradition, revealed law in the Judaeo-Christian
scriptures certainly established a law of unity and a law of trinity. Moreover, the frequent insistence on the number seven may possibly indicate
also a law of seven, or, as it is frequently referred to, a law of the octave.
This last is a misleading word; the eighth step of an octave is in fact the

---

81 James Jeans, *The Mysterious Universe*, Cambridge University Press, 1930, Chapter 5.
82 John Burnet, *Early Greek Science*, London, A. & C. Black, 4th edn, 1930, p.107. For an admirable summary of what is known about Pythagoras and his school, *see Chambers Encyclopaedia.*

beginning of the next octave. In the musical octave, for example, doh is counted twice, as both the first note and the eighth note, which in fact begins the octave next above. If there is a law of seven, it would be concerned with the seven intervals between the eight notes. This is the puzzle set by nature. In the case of the teeth of the upper and lower jaws, left and right, for example, there are apparently four octaves in two sets back to back with each other.

Scripture is very clear about the existence of these numbers in a variety of phenomena, but it reveals very little about the intention behind them, how they work, and indeed the extent to which they can be called laws. Science, however, has in the 'scientific age' of the last three centuries, since Newton, brought to light phenomena where these numbers make an intriguing appearance. It is even possible that science could have been aided in its advance by taking into account what scripture reveals. Newton was very much a religious man, but many later scientists, especially post-Darwin, have tended to lean towards atheism and to ignore scripture as unhelpful.

The Judaeo-Christian scriptures and the fragments of the early Greek philosophers bear comparison with the discoveries of modern science although the result of the comparison is a mystery which is perhaps insoluble. Nothing, however, is lost by considering the evidence. Some later seeker after truth may be able to make sense of what for the present must be regarded as mere idle speculation. The fact that no sense can be made of it today is no excuse for disregarding the interesting parallels between ancient and modern beliefs.

Unity

'IN THE BEGINNING God ...' Thus begins the book of Genesis. The old folk song puts it clearly: 'One is One and all alone, and ever more shall be so.' God is One, without a second. In Christianity this is called the doctrine of *transcendence*. Orthodoxy requires this to be held in parallel with the doctrine of *immanence*: namely that God is revealed, and can be seen to be, in everything.[83] Philosophy tussles with the perennial problem of reconciling the many with the one. Science since

---

83 See *The Oxford Dictionary of the Christian Church,* Oxford University Press, 1957, reprint 1966, under 'immanence'.

earliest times has been searching for the single prime substance of the material universe. All three seek to know how the universe can have come into being. In religion William Law (1676-1761), one of the most celebrated of English divines, pointed out that:

> It has been an opinion commonly received, though without any foundation in the light of nature or Scripture, that God created this whole visible world and all things in it out of nothing ... [and later, as to Man, he added] To suppose a willing, understanding being, created out of nothing, is a great absurdity.[84]

A solution 'in the light of nature' offered by scripture is to be found in the law of trinity.

Trinity

HOW CAN the Absolute, one without a second, transcendent yet immanent, create a universe of myriad forms? To create anything requires (1) a worker, (2) his work or effort, and (3) material to work on. The law of trinity has it that the Creator takes on all three of these roles, whilst not for one moment ceasing to be one. Christianity accordingly describes God as three persons in one substance.[85]

Indian religious philosophy likens this trinity to the three strands of a rope, constituting three forces which create, uphold and dissolve the universe.

> The creation is full of this trinity ... It is the primal factor. The same three forces are repeated all through creation to its grossest form. For example, knowledge, change and ignorance; creation, existence and dissolution; in grammar, first, second and third person, or masculine, feminine and neuter gender and so on. The pattern of three repeats right through creation from the first impulse to the very end. A discriminating man should be able to see more of it in every created form.[86]

Classical Representations of Trinity

The classical world made Jupiter, Neptune and Pluto rulers of the world; Jupiter with three-forked lightnings, Neptune with a three-forked trident

---

84 The opening lines of William Law, *An Appeal to All that Doubt*, London, 1742.
85 The vital importance of this is to be seen in the Athanasian Creed appointed in the *Book of Common Prayer* to be sung or said on fourteen special Sundays of the Christian year. Yet hardly any regular churchgoer will have heard it even once in the last fifty years or so.
86 *Good Company*, The Study Society, p.72.

and Pluto with a three-headed dog. There were three Graces, three Furies and three Harpies. Scandinavian Mythology and the Icelandic sagas purport to have found the Ruler of Aesir as The High One, The Just as High and The Third.[87] Representations of gods with three heads are common in the innumerable temples of India. But the Absolute has only one temple (at Bhuvaneshwara), and in that temple there is no worship.[88]

Examples of the Law of Three
Trinity seems to be reflected at all levels of materiality, sometimes in conjunction with or in distinction from, the one or the seven. Physicists tell us that three primary colours can be combined to form white light. Artists say these three in mixture make the variegated hues of the material world. Musicians tell us that the seven notes of the musical scale are harmonised in three major and three minor triads, which themselves give rise to secondary triads. Engineers see a system of leverage as a weight moved by a force by means of a fulcrum. All man's limbs, muscles and joints constitute systems of leverage throughout the body. Man, in the image of God, works through head, heart and physical strength, held in the three bony cavities of skull, thorax and pelvis. Can this be unconnected with law?

Language
Language has to mirror the created universe and make words to match it. It is no surprise therefore to find that the grammar of ancient languages treated all 'things' (nouns) as being masculine, feminine or neuter in gender, because in relation to other things they carry a positive, negative or neutralising force. Moreover the gender can change when the relationship changes. Hence sun and moon are masculine and feminine respectively in the Romance languages but feminine and masculine in Germanic languages. Verbs, which express action, have forms for three persons in three numbers: I, thou, he (singular); we, you, they (plural); and a dual (Sanskrit *âvâm, yûyam*; Greek νω, σφω) which has disappeared from modern languages.[89] Time is expressed in three

---

87 The Deluding of Gylfi, *The Prose Edda of Snorri Sturluson*, thirteenth century.
88 Ernest Wood, *Vedânta Dictionary*, Philosophical Library, New York, 1963, p.30, under 'Brahmâ'.
89 Singular, dual and plural forms, to express one, two or many, are found in Sanskrit, Hebrew and Greek. In Latin there is a remnant of the dual in duo, ambo and octo (eight, treated as minus two in ancient mathematics).

primary tenses, and three historic tenses, and the relic of a similar future trio corresponding to English 'I shall have been asking,' and 'I shall be going to ask.' There are three moods to express degrees of certainty; and three voices to distinguish between actions done upon another (active), done for oneself (middle) or suffered by oneself at the hands of someone else (passive).[90] Most modern languages have, of course, lost a good deal of this grammar, English more than most.

Seven Steps (the Octave)

THE OLD TESTAMENT begins with the creation of the world in seven days, which are mirrored in the seven days of the week. The 'days' in the book of Genesis are, of course, vast periods of time, as is explained in Psalm 90 verse 4.[91] Every seventh human year is a Sabbath year, and seven Sabbaths of years (49 years) is followed by a jubilee year, when all land is to be redistributed, and all who have been enslaved for debt are to be released and their debts forgiven. The seven-branched candlestick was an important symbol in the Temple. The great Jewish festivals lasted seven days with intervals of seven weeks between them.

The New Testament is no less prolific with the number seven. The Lord's prayer is divided into seven petitions. The last book of the New Testament, *The Revelation of St John the Divine*, describes seven letters to seven churches of Asia, seven candlesticks, seven stars, seven trumpets, seven spirits before the throne of God, seven horns, seven vials, seven plagues, a seven-headed monster and the lamb with seven eyes.[92] The number seven is thus emphasised again and again, but, as already mentioned, neither its function nor its meaning is explained. Science, however, has come across these numbers in so many of its discoveries that one cannot help wondering whether there is some hidden significance in the number seven.

---

90 Abbot and Mansfield, *Primer of Greek Grammar*, London, 1893, p.62.
91 The ancient priestly tradition of the Hindus calculates a day of Brahma as being 4,320,000 human years, one Mahayuga, or (in John Dowson, *Classical Dictionary of Hindu Religion, Geography, History and Literature*, 1891; London, Routledge, 2000) even two thousand Mahajugas.
92 These and thirty-three other instances of the use of seven in religion and mythology throughout the world are most usefully set out in Brewer's *Dictionary of Phrase and Fable*, under 'seven'.

The Law of Seven

It appears that the intervals between sounds which constitute a musical scale were in part measured and in part calculated by Pythagoras (582-500 BC) and his school. Using a one-stringed instrument of his own invention, he or his school are said to have reproduced a conventional Greek sequence of musical notes moving step by step from doh[93] to the doh of the next octave, at half the wavelength (nowadays more often called double the frequency). When the string was shortened by a half, the same note was produced an octave higher. A fifth higher was produced by two thirds of the length of string; and a fourth higher by three quarters of the length. The size of the seven intervals or steps between them was calculated by dividing these ratios by one another.[94] In the *Timaeus*,[95] Plato gives an account of the mathematical result of this process when carried through four octaves and a major sixth. This shows the proportions of the seven rises in tone to be 9:8, 9:8, 256:243, 9:8, 9:8, 256:243. Thus the notes of the octave rise in regular intervals of 9:8, but the regularity is interrupted in two places: after the third note and after the seventh note, where the rise is only 256:243. In modern parlance, there is a semitone between 3 and 4, and between 7 and 8, which is the start of a new octave. It will be seen later that the semitones are the vital points of the octave.

Natural Law and the Law of Nature

The learned of today are in doubt as to any connection between natural law and the law (or laws) of nature. No doubt most scientists would reject such an idea, while almost all lawyers have abandoned the whole concept of natural law. In consequence natural law no longer presents a challenge, or a bridle to the sovereignty of governments. The only bridle and challenge to sovereignty now is bureaucratic super-government from Brussels and (less successfully) public opinion.

---

93 This nomenclature was invented in the nineteenth century by a Norwich school teacher, Sarah Ann Glover, and perfected in about 1850 by the Rev John Curwen.

94 *The Encyclopaedia Britannica*, Vol. 25, p.580a sets out the calculation thus: the tone being represented by 9:8 (fifth minus fourth); i.e. ½ + ½, and the semitone by 256:243 (fourth minus two tones) i.e. ½ + (½ x ½).

95 *Timaeus*, translated by Bury, Loeb Classical Library, London, Heinemann, 1952, pp.66-72, which sets out both the Greek and the English, with very clear footnotes, using Arabic numerals. These show the relationship between the arithmetical and the harmonic mean by a different route.

If this is a correct assessment of the position, it is the exact opposite of the Pythagorean view. Pythagoras taught the doctrine of transmigration of souls and the virtue of science as a means of escape from the 'wheel of birth':[96]

> For him philosophy is not rationalist speculation on the constitution of the universe, with no bearing on conduct, but a way of life in which union or likeness with God is to be sought through knowledge ... The idea of harmony obtained by the calculation of the octave in sound was generalised in the Pythagorean school into a principle of universal application in both the material and the moral worlds.[97]

Pythagoras was largely lost to the Middle Ages except in Arabic interpretations. He was rediscovered in the Renaissance, when the theory of the octave was also discovered quite independently in China. The Chinese theory was hindered, just as was the European, by the absence of the note si.[98]

Modern Music

At the beginning of the Christian era, the Greeks were using this scale in seven different modes, many of which were adopted for church music. Additional modes, added mostly in Pope Gregory's time, brought the number up to twelve, each starting on a different note and so altering the position of the semitones, and consequently the emotional effect, or mood (mode) of the sounds. These modes lasted until about 1500, when they disintegrated under the advent of harmonised music. Ultimately only two modes remained, the Ionian and the Aeolian, which constituted the basis of our major and minor scales. Meanwhile, in the eleventh century, to make identification of notes easier for singers, Guido d'Arezzo had invented the hexachord, a series of six named notes – ut, re, mi, fah, sol, la. There were three hexachords: the hard (in the key of C) beginning on G, the soft beginning on F, and the natural beginning on C. This foreshadowed what were to become the three major chords of the octave. Of course they overlapped, so that the singer had to switch to another hexachord if the melody went outside the range of the one he was using. The French invention of the note si was needed to complete

96 John Burnet, *Early Greek Science*, pp.92ff, especially p.98.
97 Wm. Hamilton. The publisher has been unable to trace this reference.
98 Kenneth Robinson, 'Equal Temperament', in Vol. IV, Pt I of *Science and Civilisation in China*, Cambridge University Press, 1984.

the octave. Ut was renamed do or doh. The system of modes survived until Tudor times.

The manufacture of keyboard instruments, the organ and harpsichord, and later the pianoforte, caused trouble for the octave. The pitch of each note was fixed when the instrument was tuned, and could not be adapted to a change of key to a new doh. In modern terms the intervals are taken as 9/8, 10/9, 16/15, 9/8, 10/9, 9/8, 16/15. This produces two sizes of whole tone, and makes the second step and the fifth step in the octave less by a comma (a smaller step) than its predecessor. Accordingly, where the doh is altered, the intervals became irregular, and the instrument needed to be re-tuned to give a proper octave. In consequence these instruments could only be played in a limited number of keys without going seriously out of tune.[99]

The bel canto singers of the late seventeenth and early eighteenth centuries distinguished nine commas between one full tone and the next full tone. For example, A sharp was four commas above the note A, but B flat (the same key on the piano) was four commas below B, and thus five commas above A. Singers were therefore trained to avoid keyboard instruments and to sing only to the accompaniment of stringed instruments, and such wind instruments as could vary the pitch of a note sufficiently to rectify this error of a comma. The best efforts of the makers of keyboard instruments to overcome the difficulty by using split piano keys and additional organ pipes were rejected by the instrumentalists and are now only to be seen in museums. As a matter of interest, the appoggiatura originated as a means of helping a singer accurately reach a note by coming down to it, instead of going up, where the comma occurred. Later composers adopted the appoggiatura for purposes of mere decoration.[100]

There was then an alteration of the tuning to mean temperament, but this allowed composers to use only a few keys without producing a 'wolf howl' when a flat had to be played where a sharp was needed. The final result was tuning to equal temperament, which involved changing the tuning of keyboards so as to make the semitone intervals equal. This allows the scale to be used in all keys, and in all modulations, with a

---

99   See *Chambers Encyclopaedia*, 1950, under 'Temperament'.
100 Pier Francesco Tosi, *Observations on the Florid Song*, 1724, English translation 1745, Stainer & Bell, 1987.

result which, although not accurate, is not unacceptable to the human ear. In Europe, Johan Sebastian Bach (1685-1750) was the apostle of equal temperament, for which he composed forty-eight preludes and fugues, called *The Well-tempered Clavier*, covering all the major and minor keys. England was rather slow on the uptake and did not introduce equal temperament for pianos until 1846.

Physics and Chemistry

Only a few octaves of sound are perceptible to the human ear. Animals, as anyone using a dog whistle knows, have aural perception of higher octaves. When Newton at the beginning of the scientific age demonstrated the refraction of light into seven colours from red to violet, the octave had come into its own. Scientists very soon discovered octaves in the frequencies ultra (beyond) violet of X-rays, gamma, beta and alpha rays, and infra- (under) red in the frequencies of short and long wave radio. However, what is important is the irregularity of the mathematically measured intervals in the octave. These occur without doubt in the octave of sound, but have not been observed, it would seem, in any of the ultra-violet or infra-red groupings of seven. To be accurate, therefore, they should be called groupings of seven rather than octaves.

In the meantime chemists had been discovering the relationship between elements in respect of boiling points, electrical conductivity, light absorption or emission, and so on. Early in the nineteenth century Döbereiner discovered triads of elements which shared chemical properties, and these were soon extended until, in 1864, J.A.R. Newlands discovered that, if chemical elements are arranged according to increasing atomic weight, those with similar physical and chemical properties occur after each interval of seven elements. He therefore proposed a system of dividing the elements into groups of seven that had properties which were similar to the first seven elements – hydrogen to oxygen – then known. Not enough elements had by that time been discovered to establish his theory, which he called 'the law of octaves', by analogy with the musical scale. Eventually the whole range of elements proved to be divisible into groups of seven. The breakthrough came with Mendeleyev's pronouncement (discovered almost simultaneously by Meyer in Germany) that 'the elements arranged according to the magnitude of atomic weights show a periodic change of properties'. Mendeleyev predicted the existence of certain elements still to be discovered, and even described some of their properties. He drew up a periodic table of elements, leaving gaps for those which had still to be found.

The final establishment of the Periodic Table was made possible by physicists who had provided vital information from their studies of the atom. Niels Bohr had, in 1922, described the atom as a planetary system of three particles of energy with different electrical charges: the proton (positive), the electron (negative) and the neutron (neutral). This revealed the astonishing picture of the smallest known particle being of the same general form as the vast spaces of our solar system and the other solar systems of the galaxy. Electrical neutrality led to the requirement of equal numbers of protons and electrons, and hence the importance of the atomic number. In this way physicists extended the tentative conclusions of the chemists about periodicity and placed this on a firm numerical basis. The further introduction of wave mechanics explained remaining anomalies. The equivalence of the number of protons and the number of electrons was adopted as the atomic number. There remained, however, strange departures from perfection in form which can be seen in Tomkeieff's *New Periodic Table*.[101]

The physicists also sowed the seeds of doubt. Smaller particles than the three neatly arranged in the atom began to be recognised. There was talk of mesons and positrons, neutrinos and neutrettos, and also of quarks. And what about fermions and bosons, and barions, not to mention leptons? As these came to be established, 'atoms' (from the Greek for 'uncuttable') belied their name; they could no longer be regarded as the 'prime building blocks of nature'. Then in very recent years a small group of physicists began to discuss the possibility of the prime material of the physical universe being something to which they gave the name *consciousness*. This was an unfortunate choice of word because 'consciousness' has two meanings: it can be transitive, meaning conscious of something, or intransitive, meaning the opposite of unconscious. Nevertheless it was a step towards the underlying law of *unity* with which all this began. Would not *being*, ho ων (Septuagint) or το ον (Plotinus), or the Sanskrit *satya* better express what they are searching for?

---

101 London, Chapman & Hall, 1954. Have these oddities ever been compared with the harmonics of the musical octave?

This was in fact not a new idea in science. In an admirably comprehensive and well documented paper entitled *A Science Toward the Limits*[102] Emilios Bouratinos traces the history of this idea from the last years of the nineteenth century through to the present day, with intimations of it in scientists (great names such as Einstein, Eddington, Jeans, Max Planck, Schroedinger, Heisenberg, Niels Bohr) and philosophers (such as Jung, Whitehead and others). Are these, we may ask, all pointing us towards the law of unity from which we cannot escape, and which we must acknowledge if justice is to be found?

102 Apparently published privately, Athens and Oxford, 1996, 32pp.

5

Money and Banks

WE TEND TO take for granted the existence of trade, and money to facilitate it. Banks create money and money is obviously a vital constituent of trade. Yet many blame money and banking for causing many of our economic troubles, and have sought a cure for injustice in monetary reform. According to Locke, the use of money made it possible for people to enclose and retain more land than they needed. This could be interpreted as making it the Mammon at 'the root of all evil'.[103] But monetary reform is certainly not a cure for all evils. It is indeed a perilous undertaking, easily rendered ineffective by the strength of market forces. Turgot understood this. Certainly there is much to complain about in the present monetary system, but this does not mean that the creation of money should be taken out of the hands of the banking system and put into the control of government.

Money properly used is of immense benefit to mankind and there are good reasons for leaving it to develop naturally with as little hindrance from government as possible. The same could be said of the banking system. Its growth is natural and has brought about remarkable changes from time to time in the character of what can be used as money. In the last fifty years, for example, cheques, which used to be the most convenient and most popular means of discharging large sums of indebtedness, have been superseded to a very large extent by plastic cards working to computers. In the course of this magic the true character of money and the working of the banking system have become difficult to understand. Some of the old terms used, such as *loan*, *interest* and *overdraft* have ceased to describe the reality of many monetary transactions.

---

103 It is, of course the love of money that is the root of all evil (1 Timothy 6:10).

For a proper understanding of money, and of the role of banks in creating it, one must go back to basics and show how, as trade developed, money came into the picture.

The Exchange of Goods and Services

WHEN EXCHANGES take place in the first instance they are made by barter. Each party to the exchange gives something of value to the other. But the value given is never the same as the value received, for in that event there would be no point in making an exchange. This is easily understood in the case of an exchange of goods for goods.

Four Values

A man who barters apples for wine wants a certain quantity of wine and is prepared to give a certain weight of apples in exchange for it. He has two values in mind: that of the apples and that of the wine. He ranks the wine as more valuable than his apples. If it were not so, he would not make the exchange. The man who has the wine will by contrast only make the exchange if he considers the apples more valuable than his wine. His values are the opposite to the other party's values. There are thus four values to be reconciled. There may be bargaining between the two men over the quantity of wine and the weight of apples to be exchanged. The exchange will occur only if one party values the wine above the apples, and the other party values the apples above the wine, in whatever quantities are agreed. In every transaction by barter there are four values.

Money

Apples and wine are both perishable, each to a different extent, and that makes barter clumsy and difficult. But if perishable goods were to be exchanged for goods of a durable kind, the latter could be kept indefinitely and exchanged later on for other goods when convenient. Metals are durable, and of metals silver and gold are the most precious, therefore the most useful for this purpose. They have a value of their own as well as a very long life. A small weight and bulk of silver or gold is worth a great deal and they are comparatively easy to carry about. Chemistry can adjust their purity so as to standardise their value. Accordingly, goods came to be exchanged for silver and gold, which can be kept virtually indefinitely and in due course exchanged for other goods when the need arose, money forming an intermediate step in the exchange.

Money used in this way also provides a standard of measurement by which each party may assess the value of goods in which he is dealing, and compare it with the value of any other goods he might spend the money on.

Bank Money

GOLD AND SILVER were widely used as money until the nineteenth century, with baser metals sometimes used for small change. But for centuries before that, a much subtler system of money had been gradually evolving, which ultimately supplanted the use of precious metals in most mercantile transactions. The system grew up from the trading habits of merchants, from which a number of different financial institutions emerged. These flourished in their time until, during the twentieth century, their functions were largely absorbed by the banks. For purely historical reasons, the nomenclature used in banking for its various operations has become highly misleading and can give rise to serious misunderstandings of what money is and how it circulates. This causes much unwarranted criticism of the banker's role and much confusion over what are called, much too loosely, 'lending' and 'inflation'. It is therefore useful to refer to the older institutions and describe how they worked because their names matched their functions. They depended on credit and trust.

Credit and Trust

IF SAM thinks Brian's knife is better than his own, and Brian thinks the opposite, they may decide to swap penknives. Unless they trust each other, each will have to grasp the other's knife while still holding on to his own, then both must simultaneously let go their own and take the other boy's knife.

Now suppose that Sam hands his penknife over on Monday, while Brian promises to find his own knife and hand it over on the following Saturday. Here there has to be trust between the two parties. Sam, after handing over his knife, has to trust Brian, giving him five days credit to honour his promise. Come Saturday, Brian fulfils his promise and hands over his knife. The trust is released and the credit disappears. The trust and the credit are in the minds of the parties.

Next consider the case where Sam hands over his penknife to Brian on Monday in return for Brian's promise to give him a set of six conkers, two bars of chocolate and a bottle of Coke. It is difficult to assess the values of these different articles. If Brian's promise was to give services in return – to clean Sam's bike, and fetch his comic for him from the newsagent for a fortnight, it would be even more difficult to assess the value of the penknife against the value of these services. What is needed is something by which to measure value. It does not matter what is used as a measure, so long as it is something recognised by both parties. Value is in the mind of each as he gauges the worth of the objects and services. They could, for example, be measured by awarding so many points or marks out of a hundred to each object. The marks would be the measure of value.

In prison camps during the war, cigarettes were used as money in this sense of a measure of value. Among primitive peoples cowrie shells were used. In more developed civilisations it was coinage: precious metal stamped with the ruler's effigy to guarantee its acceptability. Money as a measure of value makes it possible for Sam to value his knife as worth, say, a hundred and fifty marks, while Brian thinks it is worth more, say two hundred. So long as Sam gets more than 150 he will part with his knife, and as long as Brian doesn't have to promise more than 200 there will be a sale. The price will be somewhere between those two values, and will be arrived at by bargaining between the two parties. The level at which the price will ultimately be fixed depends on the strength or weakness of the bargaining position of each.

Disadvantages of Metal as Money

Precious metal used for coinage is subject to a number of troubles, whether or not minted with an official stamp. It is awkward to carry about in large quantities. It is liable to be stolen. It can be debased by cutting away some of the metal. The coinage was debased in this way in early mediaeval times. The metal may be mixed with inferior alloys. More-over, fluctuations in the amount of precious metals coming from the mines may change their value. Increased mining produces money without there having been a sale of goods or services to substantiate it. More money is then available than there are goods and services in the market to match it. Prices have to rise to make the two match. This was observable in Tudor times, when newly discovered silver in the South American continent flooded the market with money. Gold in more recent times had to be controlled to prevent too much of it being circulated as money. The common saying is that 'too much money chasing too few goods causes inflation'. By contrast, in times of surging trade there have been disastrous shortages of precious metals, as occurred for example after the Napoleonic Wars.

Private Money

THERE IS a much better way. The parties to a genuine exchange of goods or services may make their own money to finance the transaction. They can give a promise which raises credit between them, and this credit can circulate throughout society if, but only if, there is the machinery to enable it to do so.

Bills of Exchange

The boys have grown up. Both are now merchants. When Brian buys from Sam he does not use coin, cigarettes or any of that kind of money. He promises Sam to pay the price on a certain date, say in three months time. Put into writing this is a *promissory note*, and is one type of the paper money called generically *bills of exchange*. Their use is very ancient. The Carthaginians who traded widely in the Mediterranean in Roman times seem to have used bills of exchange written on leather. The essence of a bill is that it is either a written promise to pay, as described above, or a written order on a third party to pay. One such is a cheque. If Brian gives Sam a cheque, it is an order on Barclay's Bank to pay Sam on demand the price of the goods which Brian has bought.

In fact, Brian and Sam would have no need for all this, because they know each other well, and trust each other. But here's the rub. In exchanges between people who do not know each other well enough, a buyer's promise to pay will not do. That difficulty can only be overcome if the buyer can get some well-known, trustworthy person to endorse his promise, and accept that he will pay if the buyer doesn't keep his word. This gave rise to *acceptance houses*. A great name such as Rothschild or Lazards endorsed on a bill would make a bill of exchange as good as, or better than, any coinage; better because the bill is easily carried about or posted, and can be used in lots of different countries where the Rothschild or Lazard name is known. The bill of exchange proper, after which the genus is named, is a 'written order by the drawer to the "drawee" to pay a certain sum on a given date to the drawer or to the payee'.[104] The acceptance house signs its name across the face of the bill before it is handed over in payment to the seller. Of course the acceptance house charges for its service.

Discount

But acceptance is not enough. The seller may want his money now, to buy different things in different places without having to wait for the date of payment, in three months time for example, stipulated in the bill. Moreover he may not want the particular sum stipulated by the bill but rather money in all sorts of different denominations to buy different things. To meet this need a *discount house* can take over responsibility for the bill, paying the seller in bank credit for the amount of the bill, less a discount as remuneration for the service.

Acceptance and *discounting* used often to be distinct services, but nowadays all these services tend to be offered by the big banks in addition to their older functions. These are: to take and hold in safety deposits of goods such as jewellery or deeds; to hold money for people so that it is safe; to advance money to people in anticipation of their salaries or wages or other income; and to manufacture money to enable the continued production of goods and services. In the last three of these functions, they keep an account of what they owe to their customers, or what their customers owe to them, in terms of money. Electronic banking has not changed the fundamentals of the system. The principles are the same, but are more easily grasped from a study of the history of banking.

---

104 So defined in 1579.

Banks

WHEN ORDINARY people put money into their banks, it is usually in the form of coin, banknotes and cheques. Historically, these three forms of money arose in that order. Cheques are a sort of bill of exchange, with which an ordinary person used to pay most of his debts. Notes and coin were, and still are, mostly used for small purchases. Banknotes were at first issued by all banks; they still are in Scotland. In England, since the Bank Act of 1844, the issuing of banknotes has been confined to the Bank of England.

Banks usually provide many of their services free to customers who keep a certain amount of credit in their accounts, making *bank charges* only when the customer goes into overdraft. The bank then charges *interest*. But that is actually only a correct term when the bank is lending money: for example when the customer borrows from the bank in anticipation of salary or wages, expecting to repay the loan when the pay is received.

Bank Money

An entirely different situation arises when a so-called *loan* is made to fund an enterprise. This is where the nomenclature becomes confusing. 'Loan' is the wrong word. Smith wants to start manufacturing shirts in Northern Ireland. It will be some time before he will be able to sell shirts. He has a building in mind which can be converted into a suitable factory. He has to pay builders and others to get the place ready. Then he will have to buy materials, pay staff, pay for advertising etc, etc, long before he can expect any income from the enterprise, much less accumulate enough profit to pay for all that expenditure. Accordingly, he persuades his bank manager to let him have enough money to meet this outlay, promising to refund the money when production and sales begin. The bank manager knows Smith as a trustworthy man. He examines his plans, accounts and budget carefully, and decides that the enterprise is more than likely to succeed.

The bank then advances a large sum of money to Smith, and charges him for what it is doing. The project is a success. As the money from sales eventually begins to come in, the bank is gradually repaid. Within a reasonable period the money has been repaid in full. What is this 'money'?

Money Created by the Bank

It consists of an obligation between Smith and the bank evidenced by entries in the bank's books. It may be booked as a loan account or as an advance, or as an *overdraft facility*. Smith then signs cheques. These are orders to the bank to pay his suppliers for whatever he has to buy in the course of setting up his business. To pay wages and salaries during the early days of its running, he may take out notes and coin. Each time the bank meets a cheque or hands out cash, its books show an increase in Smith's debt to the bank by the amount concerned. But what is circulating to pay for these things is a notional debt owed by the bank to Smith, of which each cheque he signs transfers a part to his suppliers etc, or, if they bank with a different bank, to their bank. At the peak of the operation Smith's account will have reached close to the maximum the bank had agreed to advance him. But thereafter Smith will be paying into the bank cheques, notes and coin received by the now flourishing business, and these will in time decrease his indebtedness to the bank until the debt is extinguished.

The vital point is that the money in which the bank and Smith deal is bank money. And this is true whether it is called a loan, an advance or an overdraft facility. These are the misleading terms. The money is created, that is to say manufactured, by the bank, and lasts only so long as the indebtedness lasts. When the debts and credits equal each other the money has disappeared. The account between them can be struck out. In essence the money they used so successfully is just like the promissory note or bill of exchange which is used between traders making an exchange. The paper passes through the hands of the buyer, the acceptance house, the seller and the discount house, where it is exchanged for bank money. The acceptors and the discounters are rewarded out of it. The bank money is used by the seller to buy things with, and those who sell to him get the rest of it and pay it into their banks. It has gone full circle.

As Professor O'Rahilly has shown, it would not have mattered if the paper with which all this started was a forgery, so long as it ended up in the hands of the forger who put it into circulation, and he gave proper value in goods or services to get it back. Only thus will the money have come full circle, supported by the exchange of goods or services for goods or services.

Definition of Money

All the variety of things that can effectively be used as a medium of exchange – bills, notes, the debts of banks and of the Bank of England – are *money*, which we can now define as a means of measuring contractual obligations incurred in trade, and of transferring them from person to person. This comes very close to the legal definition: 'the means whereby the medium of exchange or the comparative values of different commodities is ascertained. Such medium may consist of tokens or coins, which in a narrow sense are called money.'[105]

The Legal Position

The legal position is worth stating. Clearly, when a man has promised to do something in exchange for a counter-promise – to pay money, to deliver goods or to perform a service – he is under an obligation. This obligation can be extinguished in four ways. If he does what he has promised, his obligation is ended. Legally this is called *satisfaction*. Or the debtor and creditor may agree to cancel the obligation. This is called *release*. Or the obligation can be terminated by *set-off*. A owes B a sum of money, and B owes A the same amount. They can agree to set off the one debt against the other. The fourth method of extinguishing an obligation is by *novation*: substituting another obligation for it. A owes B a sum of money, and is himself owed a similar amount by C. He may be able to persuade B to let C become his debtor in his place. The debt A to B and the debt C to A are both canceled, and C becomes debtor to B. This last (novation) is the legal operation that circulates money throughout the banking system from one person's account to another's, in the same or in a different bank.

In trading, if I have bought a seat to hear a famous tenor, I expect him to sing as promised. I also expect the grocer to hand over the counter the goods for which I have paid. This is *satisfaction*. But the same is not true of a promise to pay £1,000. The creditor ultimately expects to get not

---

105 *Halsbury's Laws of England*, London, Butterworth, 2nd edn, Vol. 23, p.172.

£1,000 – that would only be an intermediate stage – but wealth and services. The £1,000 is of course never paid. The promise will be discharged by cheque, when the debtor orders Barclay's to pay his creditor £1,000. The creditor puts the cheque into his account with Barclay's or with some other bank. The cheque is met by Barclay's or the other bank recording in their books that they now owe the creditor that amount, and Barclay's reduces what they owe to the debtor by that amount. There has been a novation. If the creditor goes off and buys a lawnmower, he draws a cheque ordering his bank to pay the shop, and another novation takes place. The bank substitutes the shop for the creditor. Our creditor never wanted pounds. He was trading: that is, exchanging goods and services for other goods and services.

If any of those transactions is done with notes and coin, the position is exactly the same. Our creditor would extinguish the obligation of his debtor by taking the cash. The Bank of England's 'promise to pay the bearer' printed on the notes would now be transferred to the creditor: another novation would have taken place. Now suppose the creditor buys that lawnmower with cash, another novation occurs. The Bank of England is now indebted to the shop for the amounts printed on the notes, of which the shop has become the bearer.

Money Backed by Production and Exchange

In all this banking activity no money comes into being unless it is caused by the beginning of an exchange of goods or services. When the second half of the exchange takes place, often through a number of different people in a number of different places, the money is cancelled by set-off within the banking system. Thus the money created is throughout its life always backed by the exchange of goods and services. There is no need for any limit to be placed on the amount of money thus created by the banking system. The limit on the printing of notes is in fact an anachronism. But it would be most unwise to abolish it, because the whole structure depends on confidence.

In fact the British banking system is able to create as much money as is needed for trading, because a first class commercial bill which is not taken up by the other banks can in the last resort be sold to the Bank of England at *bank rate*. The Bank of England pays for it with bank money, which establishes a debt from the Bank of England to one of the other banks for the amount needed. All the banks have accounts with the Bank of England. They used to keep a ratio of 1 to 10, reduced later to 1 to 12, between their *deposits* with the central bank and their customers' deposits with them. Since deregulation, which has not weakened public confidence, this reserve ratio is no longer maintained by the banking system.

Deposits

The term *deposit* is of course wholly unsuitable, as is the word *interest*, to describe the debts and credits between banks and their customers, and between the clearing banks and the central bank.

A true *deposit* is made when a customer puts jewellery or deeds into the bank. This is a bailment in English law; in Roman law *depositum*. The ownership of the thing deposited does not pass to the bank and, when the bank is called upon to do so, it must return the thing itself to the customer.

Interest in its proper sense occurs only in lending. But money provided by banks in the way described above is not loaned. It is created. What the bank is paid in order to obtain it is the price of the money, a price which has to cover the bank's costs, its profit and an element of insurance against the failure both of the particular enterprise they are financing, and of any other of the enterprises they are financing.

This familiar but unsuitable vocabulary does not properly designate the banking activities described above. The terminology is a historic survival. It derives from moneylending, out of which the banking system grew.

The Moneylenders

Aaron of Lincoln, whose fortress-like house of stone is still to be seen in that city, was famous as a moneylender and, to an extent which it is impossible even to estimate, a banker. When he died in 1185 he had money owing to him in 25 countries. His customers included the kings of England and Scotland. He had provided the capital for building the abbeys at Peterborough and St Albans, and nine Cistercian houses. When he died, his estate escheated to the king, and a special department of the Treasury was set up – the *scaccarium Aaronis* – to administer his estate. The administration took twenty years to complete. This exposure of immense wealth made Jews extremely unpopular, and there was much rejoicing when Edward I expelled them from England in 1290.

Usury

The rates of interest charged by moneylenders were usually over forty per cent, in some cases as much as 60 per cent. But these high rates were for loans for purposes which were entirely unproductive. There was no trade to back them. Building an abbey or a castle does not initiate a train of production and exchange of goods and services which will in the course of time extinguish by set-off the money raised for the building. To some extent Aaron must also have been a banker, but to what extent it is impossible to estimate. But he, like the Jewish and other money-lenders in every city in England and Europe, did not charge these high rates when honouring letters of credit or bills of exchange accepted by their friends and relations all over Europe. They were then financing genuine international trade between Englishmen and foreigners. The money they created in this way would in due course be set off in the ordinary course of business.

After the expulsion of the Jews their activities as moneylenders and bankers were taken over by English merchants who by that time had become rich enough to do so. Their success in resisting the Crown's attempts to raise their feudal dues in line with the falling value of money had been very successful.[106] Some of what they were now lending to the king was in fact what they would formerly have had to pay him in dues. They were thus, to a large extent, lending the king at interest the dues they owed him!

We cannot pause to relate the other side of the story – the appallingly dishonest and savagely cruel treatment of the Jews from the Conquest up until their expulsion. They were unable to return in safety until Cromwell's time. The point we need to make is that without money-lending the huge capital programme in the early middle ages – the build-ing of abbeys and castles in particular, and the constant waging of expensive wars – could not have occurred. Wars, castles and abbeys created by capital expenditure could in no way give rise to good bank money backed by trading. The money had to be borrowed and then

---

106 See *Oxford History of England*, Oxford, Clarendon Press, Vol. III, *passim.*

dissipated. Nothing was produced in exchange for it, although the land rents seized in France by the invading English armies, and the booty they brought back with them, added a good deal to the general prosperity of some classes. The Jews lent it at high rates of interest because of the risk. In Aaron's case the risk became a harsh reality. On his death his estate forfeited to the king, and the king's outstanding debts to him were never paid. It is impossible to say to what extent the moneylenders, both Jewish and Christian, acted as bankers because the bankers and money-lenders used the same terminology.

Throughout the Middle Ages the Church, unaware of the distinction between banking and moneylending, attempted to prohibit the taking of interest. This was simply destructive of enterprise, which had to have capital. The subtle arguments of the canon lawyers gave some relief, but the fundamental error of the Church was a complete misunderstanding of what banking was about. Sensible banking practice grew up gradu-ally by trial and error without the nature of *good money* being under-stood, except instinctively, by the early bankers. Moreover, the political and social structure of the time prevented anyone seeing what caused *bad money* to come into circulation.

A Debt-ridden Society
Unfortunately, the financial system as a whole has not retained the natural controls of good banking practice. In particular, the rise in land values has been such, in the last three or four decades, that bankers have fallen into the temptation of creating money on the security of land in expectation of these rises in its value. The worst example has been the Japanese banks, which advanced huge sums of money on the security of land. When land prices dropped, and their customers defaulted, the banks found that the collapsed land prices did not cover the sums they had advanced. The money they had created was not founded upon genuine trade but upon the security against which they had made the advances. As is well known, the result was disastrous not only for the borrowers but also for the banks.

The same thing has occurred to a lesser degree in Western Europe. It was evidenced by the period of *negative equity* which ruined many who bought houses as a speculative investment rather than as a truly neces-sary dwelling. Collateral security for a bank *loan* should really be a means of obtaining a hold over the customer. The money created is only good money if its purpose is to back genuine production.

This is not the end of the story. The power of the banks to create money has also led them into competing for customers who want to borrow money, and advertising to encourage their existing customers to borrow more. This is all very well when the economy is prospering, but will lead, and has led, to disaster if and when the economy slumps. Even now it can turn into disaster for anyone who is made redundant, or otherwise loses his job or his business. In most households, not only is the house 'in hock' to a bank or building society by reason of a very large loan, but the car or cars, and some of the more expensive items of furniture and electronic gadgetry, are on hire-purchase or some similar arrangement at stiff rates of interest. The price of a car, for example is paid twice over (in capital plus interest) in a very few years, and yet a car is with very few exceptions a constantly deteriorating asset.

The result of this enormous edifice of credit is that a sword of Damocles is waiting to fall upon the debt-laden individual when his source of income is taken away, or upon the whole monetary system in the event of a serious recession. It stems from the blurring of the distinction between good and bad money.

Good Money

GOOD MONEY is money which is brought into existence by the producer of goods and services, and which serves to bridge the gap of time and space between that producer and those whose production will ultimately be exchanged for it. It makes it possible to sell production now in exchange for a claim on production in the form of money, which will pass round the community until it comes, bit by bit, full circle to be extinguished. Good money thus connects present production with the products of various kinds for which it is to be exchanged at a later date. Some will be past production which has already been turned into money; some will be future production which will in due course be turned into money; and all at different times and in different places. Throughout its life, which may be short or long, good money is backed by production. The financial (mostly banking) system as a whole allows the producer to take and use money at once. He does not have to wait for the exchange to be completed. But of course he has to pay for this valuable service. The erroneous belief that a government or the Bank of England can control the economy by setting interest rates only serves to hinder the free flow of production, and enables the banks, in spite of the genuine competition between them, to make unnecessarily large profits. Without such interference competition would reduce rates of interest to the lowest level possible.

Bad Money

Production Stimulated by Government

Bad money is a claim on production for which no production has been given in exchange. It increases the amount of currency available, without increasing production to match it. There is then 'too much money chasing too few goods'. Prices have to rise to re-establish the equilibrium. It was always known that debasing the coinage by clipping produced this result. Forgery does the same thing and the punishments for forgery were very severe for that reason. It is not difficult to see that financial expedients to fund wars were bound to have the same effect – indeed worse, for wars actually destroy some of the already existing wealth which money could have bought. Governments are the chief creators of bad money when they use money for unproductive purposes. This they tend to do all too often.

Good government, however, is a service which aids production. Peace within the realm, where the roads are safe and, outside it, where the sea lanes are kept clear of pirates, facilitates trade. Accordingly, government is productive when its efforts and expenditure produce and maintain this state of affairs. Expenditure on the armed forces, police, fire services and a host of other services are in this context productive. They increase the productive capacity of all enterprises, and in so doing increase the surplus revenue available on all lands of superior quality to land at the margin. Common sense suggests this revenue should be the property of the government whose efficiency created it. If the law, in harmony with natural law, reflected justice, it would be. If the rise in ground-rents consequent upon good government were collected by the exchequer, it would be receiving, on behalf of taxpayers, the benefit of the expenditure of their money. In this way taxation to improve public services would be a good investment because it would increase public revenue. It would be equivalent to what good landlords used to do in providing capital or encouraging new ways of working by their tenants. 'Turnip' Townshend and Coke of Norfolk in the eighteenth century are famous examples of this. They invested capital, for which their tenants paid them in increased rents. The increase in production also enriched the tenants.

Peacetime Taxation

Prior to the thirteenth century there was very little taxation for the peacetime purposes of government. There was a legal maxim that the king should 'live of his own'. In practice this meant that taxation could be levied only to finance wars and to meet national emergencies. Peacetime government had to be paid for out of the king's feudal revenues, some as an occupier of land and rather more as overlord of all other occupiers of the land of England, who paid him *dues* as well as *aids*, known as 'the incidents of tenure'. By at least the thirteenth century, the Crown's revenues as overlord of English land having drastically diminished, the magnates of the realm, lay and clerical, had to grant the Crown taxes on movables, later called *tenths and fifteenths* to make up for the lost revenue.[107] Constant warfare in succeeding reigns led to more and more taxation. The last king to promise to 'live of his own' from feudal tenures was Henry VII; and, with a certain amount of chicanery, he managed to do so. In fact he inherited an empty treasury, and succeeded in filling it to the extent of more than a million pounds before he died. Amongst other roguery he made a profit out of taxation to fund wars by making unexpectedly early peace soon after parliament had voted him his war tax. But Henry VII was exceptional. His successors sold off Crown lands to boost the revenue. Henry VIII's dissolution of the monasteries and sale of their lands helped the treasury, but only temporarily. His daughter Elizabeth was later forced to sell off land to the extent of £813,332. The rents thus lost would at today's prices be worth a very large figure indeed, which has had to be replaced by taxation. James I and Charles I completed the loss of land, making it finally impossible for the king to 'live of his own'.

---

107 Sir Maurice Powicke, *Oxford History of England: The Thirteenth Century*, Oxford, Clarendon Press, pp.28-9.

Government Borrowing

To finance government by taxation alone has almost always proved impossible. The Plantagenet kings borrowed huge sums from Flemish and Lombard banking families for their French wars. Governments everywhere, both central and local, borrowed to make ends meet. Today in England this borrowing injects treasury bills (duration one to twelve months), treasury bonds (duration one to ten years) and local government stocks into the market. These are inflationary when first put out, but not, of course, when renewed, as they constantly are. They are inflationary because they remain merely promises, never to be redeemed by production of any kind. Moreover they form a basis for the creation of more bank money. Whenever they increase in quantity, that increase is inflationary. Government borrowing by means of long-term securities has the same effect. In modern times treasury bills have dominated the money market to such an extent that they are regarded more highly than first-class commercial bills. Once their initial inflationary effect is over, they form a very useful link between the banks and the Bank of England through the discount houses as intermediaries. They are the means whereby the money supply rises and falls to meet the demand, through sales and purchases of treasury bills, allowing borrowing between banks overnight or for very short periods, and as a last resort from the Bank of England.

Social Credit

Governments are always resorting to borrowing. There have been occasions when, instead of borrowing as at present, through the banking system, and paying interest on the money borrowed, governments have issued notes directly to the public. Abraham Lincoln achieved this in America by means of 'greenbacks' of which the Treasury issued $300,000 to pay in part for the Civil War. The British government did the same, to the extent of £3.2 million, in May 1914 to finance the early stages of the First World War, with treasury notes nicknamed 'Bradburies'.[108] The effect, of course, is inflation as a concealed means of taxation. The government in fact pays a large amount of interest on public debt, and this kind of government note issue would be beneficial

---

108 Michael Rowbotham, *The Grip of Death*, Charlbury, Oxfordshire, Jon Carpenter, 1998, pp.205, 208.

if it could be instituted in peacetime without creating a crisis of confidence. But this is a very big 'if' because a monetary system of any kind is utterly dependent on confidence. A not too dissimilar national bank was instituted in France by the Scottish banker John Law, who was afterwards made the French king's Comptroller-General of Finances. In 1718 his bank in Paris became the Royal Bank, with power to issue a paper currency as legal tender. However, his grandiose Mississippi scheme to use a concession he had obtained to exploit Louisiana failed miserably, and in 1720 he had to flee the country in disgrace.

A much safer way of reducing the interest on debt of all kinds would be for governments to give up altogether the setting or controlling of interest rates. In spite of the many amalgamations there is still competition between banks, including now certain former building societies. Left to themselves, this competition would reduce to a minimum the interest they charge.

6

The Errors of Capitalism

B Y THE middle of the seventeenth century the word 'capital' had, in political economy, come to mean 'accumulated wealth employed reproductively'.[109] Although in earlier forms of society cattle, sheep and slaves were accumulated as riches and used productively, it was not until mankind turned to agriculture that goods of all sorts had to be accumulated and used *re*productively to provide tools to work the ground and food to maintain the worker during the long months which had to elapse between his sowing the seed and his reaping the harvest. The tiller of the soil was thus differentiated from earlier peoples by his need for large amounts of capital.

The first capital was provided by nature in the excess seed at harvest which was kept for sowing a subsequent crop, and in the less perishable of the earth's fruits which could provide food in the long months of waiting for the harvest. The first tools consisted of stone from the ground, or branches torn from trees of the forest and sharpened with stones. But it is by *saving* what is not immediately required for consumption that capital began to be accumulated in a meaningful way. Most such saving requires deliberate abstention from consumption.

The Growth of Capital

WHEN EXCHANGES are made for a widely recognised form of money, the recipient can keep the money for as long as he wishes, or until the need arises to buy something to complete the exchange. Trading with money is therefore a great stimulus to the formation of capital. The landowner with revenue he does not presently need can save the excess in the form

---

109 *Shorter Oxford Dictionary*, 'Capital' meaning B 2b. Pol. Econ. 1630.

of money. The capitalist who has more than he can personally use can do the same. The wage-earner too, either by discovering extra skills and other ways of saving labour, or, as is often the case, by sparing and pinching, can save money. All may contribute to the accumulation of savings, which are then readily turned into capital when borrowed by industry in return for interest.

Opposition to Money Loans

In the middle ages and up until the eighteenth century, the Catholic Church in Continental Europe campaigned vigorously against 'usury' – a term which covered taking interest on loans as well as various kinds of extortion including 'rack-renting'. But, whilst taking normal rents for land was allowed (the Church itself owned extensive estates), taking interest on loans of money was entirely prohibited.

Yet, although industry needed land on which to site its farms, factories and offices, it also desperately needed money as capital to keep all kinds of undertakings going from day to day. To assist industry in this regard the ecclesiastical *schoolmen* of the *Ancien Régime* used their casuistry to excuse the taking of interest so long as it was organised on similar lines to the taking of rent for land. The absurdity of equating immovable land, provided by nature and fixed in quantity, with the mercurial movement of the quantity of money was ridiculed by Turgot.[110] Before his time the prohibition of taking interest on loans had been so serious a handicap to industrial capitalism that one prominent writer on economics has ascribed the rise of Lutheran Protestantism in the industrial parts of Germany to industry's desperate need to borrow money for capital.[111] Although it no longer troubles the Western world, interest is still prohibited, and the same sort of evasions of the prohibition are still being used in the Muslim East.

Capitalism had been growing over many centuries in what would nowadays be considered a small way in cottage industries and merchant houses. Jews, in this as in many other things, led the way all over Europe. They were much advantaged by the Church's condemnation of 'usury' already described, from which, of course, they were exempt. The

---

110 Turgot, *Réfléxions* (1766). See Kenneth Jupp's translation, *The Formation and Distribution of Wealth*, paragraph 73.
111 See R.H. Tawney, *Religion and the Rise of Capitalism*, London, John Murray, 1926.

scientific age, by sparking off the Industrial Revolution, gave capitalism a considerable boost.

The Industrial Revolution

It was in eighteenth-century England that the accelerating development of capitalism began. Specialisation spread to every branch of production. It was only an extension of the specialisation, already described, that had earlier relieved the land worker of tasks which were better done by the farrier, the miller, the blacksmith, and so on. But now the division of labour into specialised compartments spread at first in cottage industries and later in ever more intense form in the factories of expanding towns and cities. It spread upwards into manufacturing, wholesaling, retailing, merchanting, banking, international trade, and finance. Workers were employed for wages. Cottages were superseded by back to back houses in slum streets, often in the shadow of the factory.

An important factor in this migration to the towns was the enclosure of so many villages, especially in the Midlands. The inhabitants were often ruthlessly expelled onto the highways, where they had no means of living except by crime. Turned out of their villages by the enclosures and condemned to poverty by their inability to earn a proper living for their families, many of them flocked to the towns. This necessitated poor relief at public expense, which was first instituted in England in Tudor times. As related elsewhere, imprisonment as a punishment for crime was introduced at the same time. But these provisions were manifestly insufficient to deal with the increasing poverty of the working classes of industrial Britain in the nineteenth century.[112]

Alexis de Tocqueville, who admired Britain for the liberty which was enjoyed under its constitution, did not miss the extremes of poverty and wealth which disfigured the British Isles:

> C'est au milieu de ce cloque infect que le plus grand fleuve de l'industrie humaine prend sa source et va feconder l'univers. De cet egout immonde, l'or pure s'ecoule. C'est la que l'esprit humain se perfectionne et s'abrutit; que la civilation produit ses merveilles et que l'homme civilisé redevient presque sauvage.[113]

112 See G.M. Trevelyan, *History of England,* pp.285-7 for a careful discussion of the enclosures.
113 'The centre of this foul canker is the source of the greatest torrent of human industry, which flows on to fertilize the earth. From this filthy sewer, pure gold flows. It is there that the human spirit improves and becomes brutish; that civilisation produces its marvels and that civilised man becomes nearly savage again.' J.P. Mayer (ed), *Voyage en Angleterre et en Irelande de 1835,* 1938.

The Problem of Poverty

By the beginning of the twentieth century, poverty had become a political issue. Socialist remedies, whereby state controls and subsidies relieved poverty, with higher and higher taxes needed to fund them, began to be extended and developed. By the middle of the twentieth century the concept of *welfare* or *social security* had become so firmly established that dependence on the state came to be regarded as an acceptable way of life for millions. By the end of the century there were families who had not included a wage earner of any kind for more than a generation.

The Battle of Words

Welfare and *social security* were euphemisms which disguised the true character of this attempt to relieve poverty. The proper duties of government had become confused. The new terminology implied that poverty no longer existed and that one of the principal duties of government was to provide free of charge the things that the whole population, other than the comparatively few disabled in body or mind, would, if nature were only allowed to take its course, work to provide for themselves (healthcare, education etc). The cost of administering the provision of these things on a huge scale naturally added to their expense and further increased the burden of tax.

Another linguistic assumption took hold in the case of *employment*. A man who worked without having an employer had become something of an anomaly. He was now out of place in such a society. Everybody had to be counted as either employed or unemployed. Those who were formerly independent were labelled *self-employed*. This too led to the belief that the way to enable idle people to earn a living lay in 'the creation of jobs'. A man was only free and independent if he had 'independent means' – in other words, if he had no need to work for his living! The irony of this was unseen in England. The French called such fortunate people *rentiers*.

Land Rents and Land Prices

ALL PRODUCTION has to be carried out on or from land. In itself land is only productive of wild flora and fauna. What it renders in wealth is due to the work done upon it by human labour. Anyone wanting to set up an agricultural, industrial or mercantile enterprise must of necessity find land on which to do it, and must obtain the landowner's permission to make use of that land. By convention and law the landowner charges him rent, or else (as in Britain) surrenders *de facto* ownership to him for a capital sum. The owner, as owner, need do nothing other than bargain for the best rent or price that he can get. He may, of course, do more, and many landowners sometimes do very much more. In fact one individual may play all three or any two of the roles of landowner, capitalist and labourer. The old-fashioned agricultural landlord, for example, customarily provided fences, walls, cowsheds, barns and much else of his tenants' capital, either in kind or in money, recouping his expenditure, with proper interest, in the rent. The three roles frequently overlap to a greater or lesser extent. In short, when a rent or a price is paid for land, although much of it may be due for buildings and improvements, there is always a part (the ground-rent or its capitalised price) which is due simply for permission to use the space. The amount paid for this naturally varies in line with the benefits afforded by the position of the land. It currently belongs to the landowner whether or not he plays any other part in the under-taking.

Freedom Undermined

In fact all a man needs to produce food for his family is a little suitable cultivable land and a minute capital outlay for purchasing digging and cultivating tools. A window-cleaning business requires little beyond ladders, a vehicle to carry them and space in which to store them. To set up a barber's shop or a secretarial agency, only a few square feet of land are required, but it has to be land of an entirely different kind. For these purposes, fertility of the soil is irrelevant. Situation is all-important. It has to be situated where there is custom to hand; and it will need a capital outlay for a small building or part of a building, with such equip-ment as basins and hot water, or computers and copiers as the work requires. So it is with other simple occupations.

   If all unused land, both urban and rural, were open to use in return for payment of the proper ground-rent, there would be little difficulty for ordinary people in setting up all manner of businesses from farming to financial services, especially if the ground-rent were the only taxation they had to pay.[114] But this is not the situation in real life today. The would-be worker, whether in farming, shopkeeping, secretarial services, merchanting, financial services or any other kind of work, has a formidable task in setting up even the smallest business. If he can find a property to rent, the ground-rent goes not to the Crown (in law the owner of the land) but to the freeholder who has been able in the course of our history to shrug off his own rent or dues to the Crown. The would-be worker is then faced with a heavy burden of taxes in addition to his rent, made up not just of the ground-rent but of a lease charge for the buildings too – the need for these taxes having been caused by the Crown's loss of its rents! Sometimes he will find the land he wants is for sale only, in which case the cost of borrowing to buy is added to his burden.

Secondary industries, which turn the earth's raw products into saleable goods, usually require far more capital to cover the length of time between starting to build a workshop or factory and the first sale of its products. Saving then becomes a prime necessity for a capitalist economy. Only the very adventurous – the born entrepreneur – will undertake such a perilous enterprise. First he has to discover a suitable piece of land for his purpose; next, probably through an estate agent, he has to find out who owns it. Bargaining then begins and, if the owner is hoping for planning consent or sudden demand to enrich him, he will refuse to sell, or will set unrealistic terms for the casual enquirer. The owner in any event will want paying 'up front', as they say, before any lucrative activity can begin. The entrepreneur will therefore require a bank loan at a rate of interest to match the risk entailed. Only the very brave can face it. The vast majority prefer to let others take the risks; they themselves seek employment from the risk-takers at a wage. If employment is not available, some will wait for a job to be 'created' for them by government, living on welfare in the meantime.

The Nation's Territory

Yet the land is the nation's territory. It is the space on which everyone must dwell, and from which everyone who provides for himself and his family must obtain the wherewithal to live. It is by English (and used to

---

114 This has been demonstrated to some extent in Bangladesh by Mohammed Yunus. See his book, with Alan Jolis, *Banker to the Poor,* London, Aurum Press, 1998.

be by Scottish)[115] law the property of the Crown, yet the Crown takes
no rent for its use. The French historians of economic doctrine point
out that:

> The idea of a natural right to land and a common interest in it is the instinc-
> tive possession of every nation. But in England the feeling seems more
> general than elsewhere, because, possibly, of the number of large proprietors
> and of the serious abuses to which the system has given rise. It seems rooted
> in the legal system of the nations. 'No absolute ownership of land', writes
> Sir Frederick Pollock, 'is recognised by our law books except in the Crown.
> All lands are supposed to be held, immediately or mediately, of the
> Crown, though no rents or services are payable, and no grant from the Crown
> is on record.'[116]

If the ground-rent which is now being paid to private persons and
corporate bodies were paid to the government, it would very substan-
tially reduce most peacetime taxation. It would also dispense with much
government borrowing and free the market from government interference. The banking system would then be free to create the money
necessary to cover genuine production and exchange.

Taxation

THE MAIN SOURCE of trouble is taxation, which is today not only excessive but also cumbersome, complicated, costly to collect and in certain
cases easy to avoid or even evade. It is also very unfair. The revenue of
central government comes mostly from five taxes: customs, excise, VAT,
income tax, and profits (corporation) tax.

Of these the first are also the oldest. From the earliest times customs
were a useful source of profit to owners of land surrounding a harbour.
These customary dues were taken over by the Crown in the Middle Ages.
The second was introduced from the Continent in 1643, when the
system which Dr Johnson called 'the hated excise' was imported from
France and the Netherlands on a motion to parliament by Colonel Pym.
The third, the equally disliked VAT, came in recent times from Brussels.
Excise and VAT both suffer from the grave defect that the price of the

---

115 In 2001 the Scottish parliament abolished feudal dues and invested the feudatories with outright ownership of the land of Scotland.
116 Gide and Rist, *History of Economic Doctrines*, London, Harrap, 7th edn, p.594, citing Sir Frederick
Pollock, *The Land Law*, p.12.

goods and services on which they are paid has to be raised by the whole amount of the tax. It is the final consumer who has to pay. If he happens to be a relatively poor man, the effect can be disastrous. The comparatively rich man may grumble, but he is not seriously affected by it. Income tax is usually said to date from Pitt's ministry, but was in fact instituted in the reign of William and Mary (1692 Cap. 1) to raise money for the wars with France.

It was the last of a long line of war taxes, which began with the Danegeld of Anglo-Saxon and Norman England. This was superseded by the tenths and fifteenths of the Plantagenets. These in turn gave way to the Lancastrian and Tudor 'subsidies'; and then came income tax. However this first income tax proved too difficult to collect except in the case of rental incomes, which it was impossible to hide. Accordingly it came to be known as the *land tax*!

Pay As You Earn
PAYE is an expedient device introduced in wartime which makes it virtually impossible for the ordinary wage and salary earner to escape paying income tax on what he earns. The rich, by contrast, can evade large amounts of income tax by employing accountants and lawyers to devise methods of avoidance by off-shore investment, trusts and the like. They can also, without breaking the law, charge against tax a great deal in the form of theatre seats, restaurant meals and taxi fares, and even the air fares for holidays abroad, by combining them with foreign business conferences, of which the cost is allowed as a business expense. For these the wage or salary earner has to pay from taxed income. The last straw is that the collection of income tax from the better-off depends on their living more than half the year in England, and on their honesty in declaring their income. PAYE does not allow any latitude to the wage or salary earner. In this regard he is treated as a second-class citizen.

Although income tax is the one tax which *purports* to exempt the very poor, to sit lightly upon the middle classes and to increase progressively as income increases so as to fall most heavily on the rich, it falls far short of achieving these objects. The wage earners have no possibility of avoiding a tax which they see only as a figure on their wages slip. Moreover, it is the most visible tax, and governments of any complexion strive, in their competition for popularity, to keep it low. This they do by increasing 'indirect taxation' on goods and services and production of all kinds: petrol, alcoholic drink, tobacco and so on. These so-called 'stealth taxes' take a far larger proportion of a poor man's than a rich man's income. A bottle of the rich man's expensive claret bears the same tax on its alcoholic content as the poor man's plonk.[117] To those living in remote places, petrol is a vital necessity to get to work. When they can afford only old cars, inefficient in their consumption of fuel, they require more of it than do the rich.

Crushing the Poor

The excuses made for these terrible taxes are various. They are alleged to be good for health, to reduce global warming, and to keep cars off the road and encourage the use of public transport. But these spurious excuses serve to disguise the real effect of nearly all indirect taxation, which is to make the poor poorer.

Throughout history taxation has been the bane of the poor man and the privilege of the rich. This was true of the late Roman Republic and the Roman Empire when its farmer/soldier citizens were crushed by a land tax from which the patrician class were largely exempt. It was true of the century or more before the French Revolution, when the roads of France and the transport of military equipment through each local district was provided by the *corvée* – the unpaid labour of peasant farmers. The *corvée* did not touch the nobility and the privileged who were exempt from this and almost every other tax and toll borne by the peasantry.

Feudalism

Although natural disasters such as famine and plague could not be guarded against, the intervening middle ages of feudalism were by contrast remarkably stable in their economic order. Yet feudalism has now become a term which carries connotations of privilege and oppression. It was, indeed, a system of unequal hereditary status, but its system of land tenure stood for a kind of justice. No one was so high that his landed privileges were not conditional upon the discharge of obligations and no one was so low that he was without certain rights. Although in practice it often fell short of this ideal, it was only when feudalism

117 'Plonk' is of course the First World War Tommy's adaptation of the French *vin blanc*!

began to disintegrate that privilege became wholly divorced from obligation. Those holding immediately under the Crown shrugged off their dues, while continuing to oblige those lower down the scale to render dues to them. Thus land (whether in town or country) came to be treated increasingly as *de facto* the absolute private property of head tenants free from obligation to the Crown. Deprived in this way of its land revenue, the Crown was forced to meet the expenses of government by taxes on anything other than land.[118]

Magna Carta

Justly lauded for many of its legal and political provisions, Magna Carta was a disaster for the economic well-being of the poor. The clauses dealing with scutage due to the Crown from its head tenants meant that, less than a century after the signing of the charter, it was not worth collecting. The versions in the re-issues of the charter vary. One was that no scutage should be levied greater than was levied in the time of King John's grandfather; another that no increase should be made in the level of scutage payments without the consent of the Council – the very people who paid it. This may have planted the seed of the idea 'taxation by consent', prominent in later political theory. Scutage had in any case already become a most intricate and cumbersome tax to collect, often requiring to be calculated in fractions of a knight's fee. By Richard II's time, because of the decline in the value of money, the cost of collecting scutage was more than the amount recovered. It very soon simply ceased to be collected.

Henry III

The crisis in the Crown's revenues had already become grave when Magna Carta was signed. King John, nicknamed 'Lackland' by his father, was succeeded by Henry III, who was eight years of age when he came to the throne. Only ten years after the meeting at Runnymede, the Council *'in the name of the people of the realm'* were granting him power to take one fifteenth of the movables of all the people in aid of the public revenue.[119] Ordinary people could not escape this tax, although, in

---

118 The history of English taxation is set out in Kenneth Jupp, *Stealing Our Land*, Othila Press.
119 Sir Maurice Powicke, *The Thirteenth Century*, Oxford, Clarendon Press, 2nd edn, 1927, p.29. Italics added.

spite of the wording italicised above, they had no say in granting it. After a number of different fractions granted at irregular intervals, this *aid* in due course became the regular method of taxing in the form of fifteenths for those already subject to tallage,[120] and tenths for everyone else. And so it continued until after the Civil War. The nobility were fortunate. They were usually taxed at one only of their places of residence, and partly because of their scattered manors, much of their movables remained untaxed. In other ways too, avoidance and evasion were common among the richer classes.[121]

Indirect Taxation Today

The main body of the population had, as already mentioned, no say in these arrangements. Today, however, when the ultimate control of parliament lies in the voting power of the people, the situation is worse. The price of everything sold today has of necessity to include all the PAYE of the people who made it, the income tax and profits tax paid by their employers, the fuel and other transport taxes on carriage between the different stages of the process of manufacturing and marketing, the VAT on the machinery used in the course of manufacture, and, in most cases, further VAT at the final sale to the consumer. A loaf of bread is not subject to VAT at this final stage. It is, however, subject to all these taxes, at the farm where the seed is sown, tended and harvested, and subsequently at the mill, the bakery and the shop where the loaf is ultimately sold, and it has to bear transport taxes of all kinds in the course of transit from stage to stage. Few people realise how heavily their bread is taxed.

Excise

Where excise is concerned, there is a compound element of tax when the producer has to fund the payment of the excise pending the final sale of the product to the consumer. Extra capital is needed to pay the tax before a profit is made. So widespread was the resort to these taxes that, when the customs and excise were consolidated in 1787, there were no less than 3,000 dutiable articles on which tax was collected.[122]

---

120 An arbitrary tax levied by the king on those under his immediate protection.
121 For the ease with which these taxes were evaded by the rich, see F.C. Dietz, *English Public Finance*, Vol. 2, University of Illinois, 1921, p.387; and Kenneth Jupp, *Stealing Our Land*, p.59.
122 B.E.V. Sabine, *A Short History of Taxation*, London, Butterworth, 1980, p.101.

It goes without saying that indirect taxes of this kind are costly to collect. To the extent that the money is then used for welfare payments and subsidies of various kinds to some of the very people from whom it was collected, the situation becomes even more costly, and its unnecessary complication becomes ridiculous.[123]

Tax on Employment 1999/2000

It is not difficult to work out how much an employer has to pay in tax to employ a man. Taking as an example a wage of £20,000 per annum (roughly £385 a week) earned by a single man with no mortgage, one can produce a calculation which is representative of the huge burden an employer has to bear. It is not necessarily typical or average because at each level of income and for different personal circumstances (mortgages, loans, marital status, etc) the calculation would vary considerably.

The employer gives the employee only a net wage after tax: this is the man's net disposable income, or 'take-home pay'. He never sees the rest of his wage, which is sent directly to the Inland Revenue as part of a monthly cheque to cover PAYE and employer's and employees' National Insurance Contributions (NIC). The amount due for the employee in the example would be £7,654.75 per annum.

When the employee spends his net wage, he pays substantial excise duties on tobacco, alcoholic drinks and petrol. On the majority of other items he buys he pays VAT, mostly at 17½%. These cannot be calculated, but the 1998 edition of *Social Trends*,[124] purports to show that indirect taxes as a percentage of disposable income are 31% for those in the lowest fifth of households, while the highest fifth pay only 16%. This again demonstrates how indirect taxation bears hardest on the poor. These figures may not include the PAYE, VAT and excise duties incurred at different stages in the production of items on which no VAT is charged at the final sale to the consumer.

The trade unions usually succeed in keeping up the expected standard of living of the wage-earner. Accordingly, it is the employer who ultimately has to pay all these taxes to the exchequer, directly in the first

---

123 In the budget of 2002, the Chancellor proposed increases in National Insurance Contributions upon employers in order to pay for the National Health Service. As the NHS is said to be the largest employer in the land, it will be the largest contributer to the tax.

124 National Statistics Office.

instance to cover PAYE and NICs; and then indirectly through the wage-earner as he spends his net take-home pay. In the example above, the gross wage (plus employer's NIC) is £22,440. Of this the employer pays the Inland Revenue directly £7,654.75. The employee pays £3,548.46 tax in the spending of his money. The total tax is therefore £11,203.21. If the gross wage of £20,000 were untaxed, wages of £11,236.79 would be sufficient to maintain the worker's present standard of living.

No wonder employers do their utmost to cut down the numbers they employ. It is cheaper to have the work done by independent contractors. On gross pay of £20,000, the employer's NI contribution is £2,440 and the employee's contribution £1,656.80, a total of £4,196.89. A self-employed person doing the job pays NI of only £340.60 in Class 2 or £748.20 in Class 4. No wonder the Treasury try hard to stop firms using independent self-employed people on contract. Wage-slavery suits the exchequer better than freedom. Everyone has to be employed. The nearest thing to a free man is a self-employed man!

The Basic Law

THE ABSURDITY of it all is apparent. Why then can governments do nothing about it? It is simply because they do not understand the basic economic law that all production is the result of man working on the earth, not only for its valuable animal, vegetable and mineral riches, which are materials he turns into wealth of every sort and kind, but also in these days its biosphere and stratosphere. There are many percipient entrepreneurs today who have their eye on outer space for the millions to be earned there from control of communications.

Only when governments wake up to the harm done by thousands of regulations which rob people of their freedom will any sensible impact be made on the outstanding absurdities which at present defy remedy. Instead of controlling people, governments need to control the earth's resources so that the people have access to them on equal terms. Access on equal terms is perfectly possible if everybody using any part of these resources is made to pay their rental value to the exchequer while their use continues. If government levied an appropriate 'rental' charge on behalf of society for the use of resources, the market would be the arbiter of their value. The rents received by the exchequer could replace many of the taxes now hindering every kind of human endeavour. Moreover, if rent had to be paid whether or not the land is in use, no one would be able to retain more land than he could use. There would be plenty for everybody.

The Duties of Government

NOT ONE of the various taxes so far mentioned takes into account the fundamental structure of the nation, and the duty of the government to provide space in the nation's territory on which people can dwell, and from which they can obtain a living. In consequence, the enormous cost of poor relief leads to the police and the armed services being seriously underfunded, hence to their prime duties of maintaining internal peace and external defence being neglected.

To take into account the benefit accruing to each individual and his family from the fecundity of nature (through increases in population and the natural fertility of the earth), two, and only two, collections of public revenue are necessary. One is a payment to local government by each family for their position of residence; the other is a payment to central government for the position at which they apply their industry.

Residential and Industrial

The residential rate ensures that each family pays for the benefits they enjoy from having easy access to railway stations, airports and the road system, local and national; to beautiful scenery and pleasant surroundings of all kinds; and to shops, schools, libraries, museums, theatres, cinemas – indeed to everything which estate agents when selling houses advertise as the advantage of *location*. These benefits vary widely. The rate has to be assessed according to the degree of benefit received at each particular location. 'Location, location, location' is the cry of the estate agent. It would be more suitable to hear it as the cry of the collector of the nation's revenue.

The rate upon industry makes each unit of industry pay for the advantages of its location in relation to all that the community, past and present, has provided and continues to provide – the infrastructure of roads, canals, railways and airports, and the services they are currently offering, and the co-operation presently available from the rest of the community – the availability of a workforce, the proximity of suppliers and customers, and of a large number of other services necessary to the industry. These benefits again vary widely according to location, and have to be shared equitably, so that no undertaking has an advantage over any other, but all compete on equal terms. The payment will again be according to the degree of benefit derived from the position of the workplace. It ensures what in present-day jargon is called a level playing field. It sets right the absurdity of the 'first come, first served', 'finders keepers', 'might is right' philosophy which underlies the practice, but not the law, of land ownership. By the law of England the land is owned by the Crown. Those who in practice now exercise the rights of ownership are, in English law, freehold tenants who have ceased to pay their dues to the Crown, and in Scots law were until recently the feudal superiors similarly exempted from dues formerly paid to the Crown.

Industrial and Residential Land Distinguished

An important distinction between the local and the national collection of revenue was pointed out by Adam Smith:

> The rent of land is paid for the use of a productive subject. The land which pays it produces it. The rent of houses is paid for the use of an unproductive subject. Neither the house nor the ground it stands upon produce anything. The person who pays the rent, therefore, must draw it from some other source of revenue distinct from and independent of this subject.[125]

Thus the revenue of land is only made public revenue in the case of the rate on industry. Householders pay the local rate from their earnings or savings. The original builder or developer of the land for housing may be made to pay the industrial rate, but after sale of the completed house the householder has to pay the local rate for the land from his earnings or savings from elsewhere. What is more likely, however, is that the builder or developer will have the land free for a period sufficient to complete the building, and thereafter will become liable to the local rate, the liability for which he transfers to the householder upon purchase of the house.

---

125 Adam Smith, *The Wealth of Nations*, Everyman, Vol. 2, p.324.

How to Assess All This?

FROM THE eighteenth century to the present day there is a thread of thought running through the doctrines of the economists which goes a long way towards answering this question. It was stated in the clearest and most succinct terms in the eighteenth century by the Frenchman A-R.J. Turgot: 'There is no revenue in a State which can truly be dispensed with, except the revenue from land.'[126]

Turgot explains that any tax which falls upon labour or upon capital inhibits the viability of the enterprise on which it falls. A tax on land will also inhibit production in so far as it falls on land at or near the margin. Such taxes reduce the value of what can be produced, and if the tax is large enough it will put undertakings out of business and cause desperate hardship to those formerly employed there. A rise in rates of interest commanded by or on behalf of government has the same effect. Every undertaking, if it is to continue to exist, must from year to year maintain the payment of wages, the interest on money borrowed and the profit on capital. Any encroachment on these payments is a danger to the undertaking and may put it out of business. So would the withdrawal of its capital. The revenue it pays the landowner, however, for permission to use his land is of an entirely different nature. It is not a vital necessity to the undertaking. It is a revenue which arises in the nature of things by reason of the superiority of the undertaking's location. From the viewpoint of the undertaking, it matters not to whom it is paid. They could pay the government as easily as they now pay the landowner. The viability of the undertaking would not be affected at all. Thus Turgot, along with the French physiocrats, called this revenue the *produit net*, which belongs by convention and law to the owner of the ground. To take it as public revenue is a loss only to the landowner. The industry paying it suffers no loss. It simply changes the name of the payee on its cheque for renting the ground.

---

126 *Réfléxions*, paragraph 98, translation by Kenneth Jupp, *The Formation and Distribution of Wealth*, Othila Press.

Assessment

The assessment is made today, and has always been made every time a landowner calculates the rent or selling price he can charge for his land, and bargains over it with his tenant or purchaser. Today these assessments are only made as leases fall in, and the true up-to-date rent has to be determined. It would need only a very few years to settle down into a system in which the state assesses the rent it should take. From then on reassessment would be needed each year to keep up with the very swift changes, for better or for worse, which can occur in the structure of a nation's territory. Any such change may seriously affect the advantages of particular land for particular purposes, and hence the rent that should be paid.

Later Economists

John Stuart Mill

In a chapter on rent in his *Principles of Political Economy* David Ricardo noted the assistance given by the convenient situation of land. John Stuart Mill understood the necessity of collecting this advantage as public revenue:

> Suppose that there is a kind of income which constantly tends to increase without any exertion or sacrifice on the part of the owners, these owners constitute a class in the community whom the natural course of things progressively enriches consistently with complete passiveness on their own part. In such a case it would be no violation of the principles on which private property is founded if the State should appropriate this increase of wealth, or part of it, as it arises. This would not properly be taking anything from anybody; it would merely be applying an accession of wealth created by circumstances to the benefit of society, instead of allowing it to become an unearned appendage to the wealth of a particular class. Now this is actually the case with rent.
>
> The ordinary progress of society which increases in wealth, is at all times tending to increase the income of landlords; to give them a greater amount and a greater proportion of the wealth of the community, independently of any trouble or outlay incurred by themselves. They grow richer, as it were in their sleep, without working, risking, or economising. What claim have they, on the general principle of social justice, to this accession of riches?[127]

127 J.S. Mill, *Principles of Political Economy*, Book V, Chapter ii.

The first step, Mill said, should be a valuation of all land in the country. Then, after an interval, 'the increase in value should be estimated and be taken as land-tax, which for fear of a miscalculation should be considerably within the amount thus indicated'. If this recommendation had passed into law in the nineteenth century, one can imagine the immense relief from the burden of taxation which would have been achieved by the end of the twentieth century, especially having regard to the savage inflation caused by two world wars. In fact things have got so much out of hand since then that more drastic measures are now necessary. But Mill's scheme at least indicates the framework. 'Those who appropriate to themselves the use of the resources of nature should pay the rest of the community for the privilege they enjoy'.

Henry George

However, when dealing with this problem the political economists had had in mind a mainly agricultural model. It was not until Henry George published his *Progress and Poverty* in 1879 that the sheer superiority of contact with the human environment as the cause of rising land values was made apparent.

George described the hard life of the first settler in the American West arriving in a territory inhabited only by Red Indian tribes. The difficulty of choosing the precise spot in which to settle was immense but only because of the wealth of natural riches. 'Tired out with the search for one place that is better than another, he stops – somewhere, anywhere – and makes himself a home.' Not so the second family to arrive. 'Though every quarter section of the boundless plain is as good as any other section, he is not beset by any embarrassment as to where to settle ... He settles by the side of the first comer.' The two can work together to undertake jobs which were beyond the strength and resource of one family. The two families are then joined by others until first a village is formed, then a town, and ultimately a city, in which the piece of land chosen by the first settler becomes, through no fault of his, nor by any effort on his part, the central square surrounded by offices and shops yielding large sums per square foot in ground rents.[128]

---

128 Henry George, *Progress and Poverty*, a précis of part of Book IV, Chapter 2.

The Growth of Population

What lies behind this remarkable insight is that the power of the community acting in concert becomes more and more important, while the power of the earth's largesse becomes less and less important as population grows, and the different levels of society are formed, from remote hamlet to teeming city. The first of these powers is, of course, the result of man's being 'by nature a political animal' (Aristotle), or 'formed for society' (Blackstone). The two powers, however, are not by any means unconnected, or even separate. Indeed they are two limbs of a trinity. The expansion of world population (it almost doubled from 1.5 billion in 1850 to 2.5 billion in 1950) is brought about by the power of nature, which is also the power behind the fertility of the soil. This is a truth which cannot be satisfactorily grasped except from a metaphysical viewpoint. It can be glimpsed by a poet, as is shown by the passage from Dante cited earlier, but science is blind to it. In these materialistic days any science which pretends to a metaphysical dimension is likely to be rejected. Nevertheless, it is a plain fact that the Creator (whoever or whatever he or it is)[129] made the planet earth with all its animal, vegetable and mineral riches, and the human race to people it. The land they inhabit sustains their life, and from the resources of the planet they create their artificial world of hedgerows and plantations, streets and houses, cities and temples. Until it is recognised that land is a vital necessity for every family in the nation, and that the revenue from land is the natural public revenue, there is no hope of releasing the people from the servitude of dependence on the state for a livelihood they could well provide for themselves if only they were given the freedom to do so. Poverty today is attended by much poor relief – but the aim of government should be the abolition of poverty, not its relief.

Taxes on Production

The practical effect of taxing everything, other than the revenue from land, is to enable those who work on land which connects them with the largest numbers of mankind – for example, from a Lombard Street office – to earn bonuses of £1 million or more,[130] while those on

---

129 'O, God forasmuch as without Thee / We are not enabled to doubt Thee, / Help us all by Thy grace / To convince the whole race / We know nothing whatever about Thee' (Ronald Knox).
130 This was the level of bonus in fact paid to a number of operatives in the City at Christmas 1997.

farms 'out in the sticks' cannot make ends meet even with the help of government subsidies. Indeed these subsidies put up the value and price of farmland, thereby helping only the farmer who owns his land, and the farming tenant's landlord. They are land subsidies rather than farm subsidies.

Taking the surplus production from the valuable land in the city by means of a rate on industry would establish an equality between the centre and the margin which would be beneficial in itself. It would also bring about a decline in the price of goods of all kinds because the revenue collected in this way would enable the indirect tax element in prices to be eliminated. The reduced prices would reduce the size of welfare payments. This in turn would reduce taxation still further. Throughout these changes, the revenue from the location of land would be increased. But this, far from doing harm, would enhance the size of the public revenue, and further relieve taxation.

Land Revenue or Taxation?

TO REPLACE peacetime taxation by rent paid to the Crown by its freehold tenants would require a survey of the nation's land on the lines of the Domesday Book. This is not as daunting a task as it might seem. William the Conqueror's survey in 1085 took only twelve months to complete. Today it could be done without the journeys on horseback to each district, the swearing in of juries to collect the necessary evidence, and the collation of it with pen on parchment. The task is far less formidable today, and keeping it up to date each year thereafter with the help of computers, fax machines, telephones and aerial photography, would be child's play.

The benefits to society of making this switch are many:

- **1** If the owners of land lying idle, whether in town or country, had to pay a proper rent for it, they could not afford to keep it idle for long. They would either have to put the land to work to make it pay the rent (possibly by finding a tenant to do that for them) or else abandon the land.

- **2** Given the opportunity to rent abandoned land, or offer themselves as sub-tenants of land lying unused, people would be able to start small businesses requiring only moderate capital outlay, without large bank loans and mortgages. They would step out of the welfare state, and take others with them as partners or employees.

- **3** With every reduction in those dependant on welfare, indirect taxation, which forms part of the price of goods and services, could be reduced. This would increase the real value of money wages, so that wage earners would actually receive more without being paid more. Lower prices are not only a relief to the population in general, they also make welfare less expensive, and reduce the costs of businesses.

- **4** Because rental values would be established by market forces and would be public knowledge, tax avoidance or evasion would be impossible – land cannot be moved to tax havens, and failure to pay would terminate the tenancy.

- **5** The 'black economy' would also disappear. It is the product of our present tax system based on income rather than location.

- **6** Against the cost of setting up the system initially should be set the very substantial saving every year in the cost of collecting existing taxation through the Inland Revenue and Customs and Excise. Much of this machinery would become redundant.

- **7** Once taxation shifts from people, their industry and their capital, onto land values, the present vicious circle (poverty – more welfare – increased taxation and borrowing – a greater burden on industry – and so more poverty) would end. It would become a virtuous circle in which relief from taxation reduced prices – demand increased as people bought more – production increased – higher profits were untaxed – and the value of superior land increased, putting more revenue into the exchequer.

Natural Law

IT IS IMPOSSIBLE to believe that the Almighty, having created man for society, had not foreseen its needs and provided in the natural course of things a means of funding them. The revenue from land is by nature the revenue of society. It comes into being naturally when society begins to take shape. Its size increases in step with the increase in the size of the society which creates it, and diminishes when the work of society in any way slackens. Thus it is that, in closely integrated societies with large populations, incomes in farming, which depend chiefly on the powers of nature to aid labour, inevitably fall far behind the incomes in service industries, which depend more on the power of society. That is why farmers are in such difficulties today. Were ground-rent to become the basis for government revenue, this shift would automatically relieve farmers of the present tax burden, making unnecessary the present subsidies which distort prices and world trade.

7

'Justice standeth afar off' [131]

Errors of Capitalism Led to
the Errors of Socialism

T HE LAST two centuries have seen a bitter struggle between capitalism and socialism. After the First World War Russia, with characteristic thoroughness and ruthlessness, instituted Communism, an extreme form of universal socialism. This was seen as the panacea for all ills. Its influence spread rapidly amongst radical thinkers in other parts of the world, even to the extent of provoking intellectuals of many nationalities to plot the downfall of their own countries. By the end of the Second World War its influence was such that socialist measures were bound to be adopted at least to some extent in most countries. Ultimately, Communism failed, but its failure became unmistakable only when, long after the death of Stalin, the system was eventually relaxed under President Gorbachev. The previous seventy years of the strictest possible socialism were at long last shown to have been a disaster.

Capitalism has not yet been fully tested in this way. Moderate socialism continued to be popular in spite of the collapse of Communism. Capitalism has never been adopted for very long in such an uncompromisingly complete form as was Communism. Even the most right-wing governments have continued to legislate on socialist principles in many spheres. The language and aims of socialism, one might say, dominated the argument for most of the twentieth century.

131 Isaiah 59:14.

Flaws in Capitalism

In its early days capitalism was dragged down by the insouciance of those who held the land. They were able to demand payment for allowing it to be used for productive purposes. The aristocracy and the Church, in ignorance of the Creator and blind to the sin of 'I, Me and Mine',[132] were content to make money from controlling this essential means of production. Without permission to use land, no production was possible. The landowner stood between the entrepreneur and access to the gifts of nature, the land itself, which the entrepreneur and his labourers needed to work on. The landowner had to be paid. Until the middle of the nineteenth century, capitalism was further burdened by protectionist tariffs which prevented free trade, and by government restrictions aimed at relieving poverty. The Church failed to insist on the Torah's message that 'the earth is the Lord's and the fullness thereof'[133] – the fullness which is the Creator's providence for the livelihood of all mankind (and that includes everybody!)

France

When capitalism was beginning to grow in eighteenth-century France, the French nobility and Church burdened it with inordinate demands to satisfy their greed, their vanity and their disdain for the lower classes. Atheism was prevalent among many of the higher dignitaries of the Church. Alexis de Tocqueville observed 'how irreligion had become a general and dominant passion among the French of the eighteenth century'.[134] Most of the nobility were little interested in the poverty of the general population. They were content to enjoy the internal tariffs they levied at district boundaries, where they themselves paid no tariff, and to force the peasants to provide free labour for the *corvée*. Revolution, although its causes could have been reformed, soon became inevitable, and this destroyed all hope of freedom until the 'genius without morality'[135] of Napoleon came to the rescue and instituted a new society organised on military lines intent on France's *jour de gloire*. The Napoleonic influence has never been entirely abandoned, even in

---

132 See *Theologica Germanica,* Chapter II.
133 Psalm 24:1.
134 *L'Ancien Regime,* Oxford, Basil Blackwell, 1949, chapter heading p.158.
135 Alexis de Toqueville's description of Napoleon.

modern France. Capitalism there is still handicapped by many national institutions which are run on semi-military lines to produce goods or services, and which, lacking the restraint of religion, are easily turned into a system of greed and egotism.

Great Britain

Great Britain fared a little better. The suffrage was, however, capped by a property qualification which was beyond the reach of the poor. It took three Reform Bills, spread over the nineteenth century, to give the people power to elect the House of Commons, and a fourth in the twentieth century to make the suffrage universal. Unfortunately, the succession of bills achieved this only by gradually abolishing the property qualification. It would have been better done by abolishing poverty so as to spread the property qualification more widely! As it was, in the final result, the stricken lower classes were left with a vote, but without a stake in the national territory or in the structure of society which would give them good reason to feel responsible for its welfare.

Meanwhile devastating poverty at home was both masked, and to some extent relieved, by the demand for expatriate enterprise and employment throughout the expanding Empire, and indeed elsewhere abroad. At home, the abolition of the slave trade, the repeal of the corn laws and the reform of prisons, of public executions, of child labour, of safety in mines and factories, and many other worthy causes, kept the reformers busy with piecemeal social improvements. In the last years of the nineteenth century, Irish self-government came to be the dominant political issue. There seemed to be no time left to address the basic injustice whereby millions of people, not only in Ireland, had some power to control government by their votes but no means of earning a living wage. Not unnaturally, they welcomed the promises of a socialist system, free provision by government of the necessities of life – education, health care, pensions and so on – which their inadequate wages could not possibly afford. The consequent loss of independence and self-reliance went unnoticed. Needless to say, the burden of taxation to pay for the provision of these necessities became increasingly hard for all classes to bear. By an absurd circularity this burden has ultimately come to bear hardest on the poor, whom it was meant to benefit. Indirect 'stealth' taxes confiscated a larger proportion of their income than that of the wealthier classes, and income tax was deducted from their wages before they were paid.

Throughout the nineteenth century, capitalism was in chains. From the start ground-rents and royalties were skimmed off by landowners before any capitalist enterprise could be undertaken, and entrepreneurs were forced to put extreme pressure on labourers of all ages to work long hours for the lowest possible pay. They were able to recruit labour, even on these harsh terms, simply because the landless, who had flocked to the town slums following the enclosures, were plentiful enough to be forever competing for work.

A further handicap in the first half of the century was the system of protective tariffs. Only when the movement for free trade began to succeed was this obstacle cleared. By then the appalling conditions of labour in mines and factories had begun to shock public opinion, forcing governments to impose controls to alleviate them. Socialism began to look attractive; but the incipient imposition of government controls put further chains on capitalism. The working classes were already demoralised and antagonistic. Class warfare became inevitable. Capitalism never had a chance.

In addition to these evils, some entrepreneurs realised that, if they could buy out the landowners instead of renting from them, they would avoid the ever-increasing drain of rent and add land-revenue to their profit. But it was a risky business. Large sums had to be borrowed at high interest rates in order to buy the land. When these borrowings swamped the entrepreneur's profit, there were many bankruptcies, which in those days caused disgrace and much suffering. However, entrepreneurs who succeeded in capturing the land revenue were able to work without having to earn true profit, while those who obtained the land revenue and also made profits became wealthy enough to buy out less successful enterprises and thereby monopolise markets.

The Twentieth Century

The early part of the twentieth century saw the growth of even more desperate socialist measures, by then sorely needed, to relieve poverty. Some speeches of Winston Churchill, as a cabinet minister 1908 to 1911, urging the abolition of poverty and not just its relief, sank into oblivion as he turned to play a considerable part in meeting the dire emergency of the First World War. After the 1918 armistice, widespread economic distress and industrial unrest were followed by a neglect, indeed a refusal to re-arm, which Churchill attacked from his political wilderness of the inter-war years. German preparations for further aggression were ignored until it was too late. Britain and its Empire were projected, almost entirely unprepared, into the Second World War of 1939-45.

Capitalism was by now believed to have failed totally. During the war, propaganda issued to the troops through ABCA,[136] promised social security to support the needy 'from the cradle to the grave'. After the war it was hailed as the only remedy. Yet capitalism had not really totally failed: it had simply been poisoned by an unjust treatment of land ownership, thwarted by misguided government. It had never been unfettered. It had never been open to competition on terms of true equality between enterprises, and had consequently come to be regarded as inherently unjust. Moreover, the tide of government interference, with heavy taxation to finance it, had only just begun. In the years following the Second World War this tide came in like a flood. More and more shackles were placed upon capitalism. Undertakings which got into difficulties were taken over by more fortunate companies which manoeuvred themselves into positions of monopoly. The establishment of a Monopolies Commission did little to curb their activities. The real beneficiaries of monopoly regulation were lawyers and accountants.

In the last decades of the twentieth century the stranglehold of legislation from Brussels and Whitehall made life increasingly difficult for small businesses, while multi-national giants swallowed up more and more companies which they directed from a distance, in which their interest was purely financial. The entrepreneurs in their subsidiary companies, often engaged in a variety of different businesses in more than one country, were employed by the financiers as servants. The huge conglomerates were managed by accountants, tax consultants, commercial lawyers and experts in public relations or advertising. This is still the case. With their real skills in international organisation, they can take raw materials from one country, have them processed in another, transported by another nation's shipping, and marketed in yet another. Prices between their subsidiary companies, as the goods go from one stage to

---

136 The Army Bureau of Current Affairs, which junior officers who had to instruct the troops in it will remember.

the next, are arranged artificially so as to avoid high taxation in one place, high wages in another, or government restrictions, tariffs, exchange rates and other impediments anywhere along the line. By so doing they distort trade, destroying, both at home and abroad, whole industries which could otherwise provide perfectly satisfactory goods for their own countries. They add unnecessary traffic to the roads, sea lanes and air routes of the world, their revenues being sufficient to absorb these vast transport costs. A change of policy by such an organisation can at a stroke abolish tens of thousands of jobs in different parts of the world. They can trade upon the ardent desire of governments in different countries to get factories or offices built to create jobs for the unemployed. They can force governments to subsidise them, to give them 'tax breaks' and other forms of special treatment by refusing to build without these privileges, or, when established, by threatening to move elsewhere on the international scene if their wishes are not met. Corrupt payments by these corporate giants are increasingly being uncovered.

What of the Future?

Natural law has been a dying concept since at least the middle of the nineteenth century. A proliferation of tribunals now deal with claims for remedies which stem, not from the common law of England, but from legislation to deal with a variety of minor ills that a shackled capitalism creates. Large damages can be obtained for oppression of one kind or another resulting from the sheer stupidity of the system. The Royal Courts of Justice appear to many to be ill-named – in reality they are courts not of justice but of law. The simplicity, indeed beauty, of the common law has been overshadowed by a tangle of statute law, and a proliferation of statutory rules and orders, exacerbated by some three thousand EU directives emanating from Brussels each year.

To apportion blame is no help to anyone. The only proper prayer in the circumstances is: 'Forgive them, Lord, for they know nor what they do.'[137] Edmund Burke showed the way:

> It is the business of the speculative philosopher to mark the proper ends of Government. It is the business of the politician, who is the philosopher in action, to find out the proper means towards those ends, and to employ them with effect.

137 Luke 23:34.

Imagine lawyers returning to Blackstone and rediscovering natural law; the Church 'searching the scriptures'[138] and rediscovering the Torah concerning land; the universities looking again at Cardinal Newman's view of a university as 'a place of teaching universal knowledge ... [with] the Church necessary for its integrity'.[139] Finally, dream of a time when politicians become sufficiently humble to seek the fundamental cause of our troubles from Church, university and law thus reformed, and explore practical means of putting into effect the resulting revelation! The only answer is humility and truth-seeking, first by serious-minded individuals, then by society as a whole.

A Memorial of Time Past

An English village is now much sought after: by the rich as a week-end home, by the less well-off as a permanent place of retirement, and by many of all classes as a retreat for the few weeks of their annual holiday. 'The Manor', 'The Grange', 'The Rectory', fetch fancy prices. Local inhabitants are being squeezed out by increased competition for country dwellings. Villages provide attractive backgrounds to many detective novels. They are memorials to what we are losing.

The typical village is centred upon a church. When, in medieval times, villages grew by establishing colonies, the satellite villages were often called after saints in the manner of Terrington St Clement, Terrington St John and Terrington St Mary Magdelene, and each soon acquired its own church and own 'big house'. In the ancient universities, college buildings are clustered round a chapel. By contrast, modern university buildings tend to be grouped round the canteen, and many a caravan site is centred on the lavatories!

Taxation Today

Farming

The farmer provides a prime example of unjust taxation. All farmers are taxed equally – which in itself is absurd since the hill farmer has far fewer resources from which to earn his precarious livelihood than has a farmer in the fertile plains with the custom of large towns close by.

---

138 John 5:39; Acts 17:11.
139 John Henry Newman, *The Idea of a University*, 1854.

Farmers, whether rich or poor, pay the same taxes as townspeople. Yet the same effort and skill applied in town or city produce immensely more wealth, and more quickly, than farming ever could. How much does a farmer make out of a crop of corn or grazing for stock? Whatever his profit per acre may be, and of course it varies considerably according to the quality and location of the land, it does not compare with the £1 million or more per acre he might make if he could get planning permission to produce a crop of houses.[140]

In the course of the last century, as Britain has become more and more industrialised and urbanised, farmers have become increasingly marginalised. The large number who managed to buy out their landlords were not so badly hit. After the First World War, however, farming became an industry for the poor, and after the Second World War even substantial subsidies failed to revive it. The effect of the subsidies was to increase land prices, which benefited farmers who owned their land but helped tenant farmers only temporarily. Today the pressure of Common Agricultural Policies emanating from the EU is dealing the death blow to genuine farming in England. Many would-be farmers are abandoning their true occupation and resorting to holiday homes, exhibitions, farm shops and other gimmicks to make some profit from the land. Fishing has suffered even more drastically.

This is the unavoidable result of failing to tailor taxation to the resources from which it has to be paid. Taxes such as income tax are supposed to match the ability to pay, but this is taken to mean the amount people have in fact earned and results in burdening people who work harder than others, while lightening the load on those who take life more easily. The proper criterion of 'ability to pay' should be the benefits afforded by society which increase people's ability to earn.

Railways

The railways have been placed since their inception in an invidious position. The capital expenditure necessary in their building was enormous. It is extraordinary that their construction could ever have been attempted and that, leaving aside the many bankruptcies, the ambitious projects could ever have been completed. The trouble was that the railway-

---

140 This is the current figure in south-east England. Of course it varies with the location of the land and is considerably lower in the north.

builders were denied the huge rewards created by their capital invest-ment: these went to the owners of land on both sides of the line whose property, especially when near a station, increased in value because of the existence of this new form of transport. Thus the landowners obtained the revenue generated by the railway while the promoters were left with the impossible task of recouping their capital expenditure out of fares. The income from these was always sufficient to pay for running costs and maintenance but, no matter how high the fares were set, they could never recoup the capital, much less pay for modifications and improve-ments to the line. In the event, the railways had to be subsidised, then nationalised, and then privatised again with substantial subsidies from the taxpayer. They were never able to reduce fares to a level where travel by rail is cheaper than travel by road, especially for two or more passengers travelling together.

Paying for Public Works
The principle that landowners who benefit from the capital outlay on works of a public nature should pay towards the cost of their construc-tion was perfectly understood by parliament towards the end of the nine-teenth century. In the Public Street Works Acts of the 1890s, for example, the cost of paving urban streets, and in the Land Drainage Acts of the 1920s, the cost of draining fens and other waterlogged land, was collected from the surrounding landowners according to 'the degree of benefit' they received by reason of the works. It was the application of the principle described above. By that time, however, the railway system was nearing completion, and only a few new lines would have been able to benefit from it. In recent years, when the railways were being expanded and developed to take faster and more frequent trains, the principle seems to have been forgotten, with disastrous consequences.[141]

Motorways
The same absurdity is to be seen in the construction of motorways. The capital cost is borne by the exchequer, that is to say by the taxpayer. But the new motorway redounds to the benefit of some and to the detriment

---

141 The principle has been vividly described by Don Riley in relation to the Jubilee Line underground rail-way in *Taken for a Ride*, London, Centre for Land Policy Studies, 2001.

of others. On one hand the supermarket, the large do-it-yourself store and one or two other retailing giants are able to obtain sites at agricultural prices near a motorway junction, where at considerable profit to themselves they capture the trade which used to sustain the shops in the surrounding towns and villages. On the other hand the High Streets of villages die a natural death as the car-owning population take to supermarket shopping. Moreover the advent of the motorway may spell death to the filling station which had flourished on the trunk road the motorway replaced. Landowners suffering from new public projects such as this are usually entitled by statute to compensation for their losses. In one such case reported in the press, the garage owner, very properly, received over £4 million in compensation for lost profit. What was improper was that the legislation made no provision for the beneficiaries of the new motorway paying for their gain, so the taxpayer had to foot the bill for the compensation as well as for the building of the motorway, while the beneficiaries of the motorway made very large gains. The law as it now stands is that you are compensated for the detriment caused by such a project but you pay nothing for the benefit received from it. This is plainly unjust.

Governments today introduce, at considerable administrative cost, 'initiatives', 'regeneration programmes', 'employment and education action zones', 'enterprise grant areas' and other measures for the relief of poverty, which serve only to increase taxation by providing subsidies, and to demean and devitalise the recipients of the subsidies. A simple act of parliament allowing the exchequer to collect the annual rise in the value of land brought about by the execution of public works would rid us of most of these showy but ineffective initiatives.

Natural Law
Law, if it followed natural law, would demand that each individual pay the nation for however much of the nation's territory he takes for his own exclusive use. To take from the universe more than one needs of anything breaches the commandment 'Thou shalt not steal'. To enclose land and not use it is indeed theft. It is stealing from a section of mankind their God-given birthright of space on the earth's surface on which to make a home, and from which to have access to the animal, vegetable and mineral bounty of nature, and the society of neighbouring human

creatures. This could not happen if all land had to be paid for, whether used or not.

The Effects of Both Capitalism and Socialism

WHILE THE nation's revenue from land is allowed to accumulate in the hands of private individuals or companies, those in superior locations can use their land revenue to reduce or even eliminate their profits while they price their products below the level at which their less well placed rivals can remain in business. When this policy drives a rival into difficulties, they can buy him out at a bargain price and take over his custom. If they decide to close down the rival's business, the owners (in large firms, the shareholders) are well rewarded, but the wage and salary earners lose their jobs and have to be content with redundancy pay, to which they are entitled by statute.

The business pages of the newspapers week by week are full of the wrangling and bargaining between large companies and international traders taking over or resisting takeovers of this kind. Satisfied shareholders heave a sigh of relief. Directors retire on large pay-outs. Trade unions boast of having obtained good terms for their members. The subsequent gradual but steady loss of jobs which then takes place over a period of time is no longer news, except to the unfortunate losers of those jobs. Few people appreciate that history is repeating itself. The losers are the landless who have no livelihood except by leave of those who have unfettered control of the land.

The buying and selling of businesses goes on while wage and salary earners toil in the hope of not losing their jobs. A German firm takes over a British firm amid resistance from British public opinion; British firms take over German firms against similar resistance from the German public. All over the world this process goes on, with the helpless workers being shifted to new owners as if they were slaves. Then, precisely because they are not slaves, and the owners have no responsibility for them beyond the duration of their jobs and a period of redundancy pay, they are dismissed into unemployment. They are only wage-slaves.

That over a thousand years of advance in science and technology should have produced no greater freedom for labour is something which requires investigation. Why are ordinary people so little better off? Are they indeed better off at all? Direct comparison is impossible, but one thing is beyond doubt: if science and technology have enabled the labour of a man to be even a hundred times more productive than it was ten centuries ago – and the proper figure for multiplication must surely be bigger than that – then today's labourer is most certainly not a hundred times better off. By contrast, in 1998 America's top executives saw pay rises of 36 per cent, while production workers got 2.7 per cent. By the end of 1998 top bosses earned around £6.6 million a year. Workers earned on average £18,000.[142] Where is the justice here?

Criminal Justice

Imprisonment

The state of our prisons is deplorable. They are expensive, overcrowded, riddled with drugs, and a corrupting influence on first-time inmates. There are even prisons which are ruled by drug barons. Imprisonment as a punishment gives rise nowadays to considerable controversy. Some think it is the only proper punishment for serious offences; at the very least it keeps the criminal from crime for a period. Others suspect that the prevalence of crime in society today is due to poverty and prefer to keep the criminal out of prison by a variety of social remedies intended to reform. Suspended sentences, probation, care orders and devices such as training schemes are now in vogue, but they are clearly failing to reverse the upward trend of crime.

What seems to have escaped notice is that imprisonment imposed by courts of law as a punishment for criminals is of remarkably recent origin. Of course *private* prisons have been used throughout history by powerful individuals who wanted to be rid of enemies or rivals! Every mediaeval castle had its dungeons for the incarceration of enemies, and indeed for the punishment of idle serfs. But this was nothing to do with courts of law.

Earlier Punishments

In early times, traitors were treated as enemies and put to death with or without trial, but for other crimes, even murder, death was a rare

142 See *Daily Telegraph*, 31 August 1999.

sentence. Banishment was the ultimate punishment. Fines and forfeitures were commonplace and brought substantial revenues to the Crown. The mediaeval courts, far from costing money, were a source of considerable revenue. In Plantagenet times, when the king took over the local jurisdictions, receipts from 'fines and amercements' in the king's courts brought in revenue, dubbed a *magnum emolumentum* of the Crown. By Elizabeth's reign, the introduction of imprisonment had reduced the income from the royal courts to about £2,000, although in those days even that was not a small sum. It should certainly make one wonder how such a lucrative system could have turned into the considerable drain on the exchequer caused by the administration of justice today. Legal aid alone is currently costing over £2 billion. The flow of money should be from the criminal to the Crown, not from the Crown to the criminal. A little more light could be shed on the debate by a consideration of legal history. How did this change of direction come about?

After the Royal Courts were established through the circuit system in the reign of Henry II, the king's judges sent on circuit used imprisonment as a means of ensuring the presence of the defendant at the trial, and of compelling obedience to orders of the court. All over the country they assumed power to imprison indefinitely after conviction, but it swiftly became their practice to use this power to extract money from the defendant:

> The justices do not want to keep him in gaol, they wish to make him pay money. [After 1215 they had no power to fine. The imposition of a fine would have been an evasion of Magna Carta.] What the judges can do is this: they can pronounce a sentence of imprisonment and then allow the culprit to 'make fine', that is to say make an end (*finem facere*) of the matter by paying or finding security for a certain sum of money. In theory the fine is a bilateral transaction, a bargain; it is not 'imposed' it is 'made' ... The wrongdoer rarely goes to prison even for a moment. On the plea roll the *custodiatur* which sends him to gaol is followed at once by *Finem fecit per unam marcam* (or whatever the sum may be), and then come the names of those who are pledges for the payment.[143]

The statutory use of imprisonment as a means of punishment came largely as the result of enclosure. The Statute of Westminster, 1275 (Chapters 9 to 32) imposed short terms of imprisonment to be served in

---

143 Sir Frederick Pollock and F.W. Maitland, *History of English Law*, Cambridge University Press, 2nd edn, 1923, Vol. 11, p.517.

local lock-ups for some half dozen offences. Of these Chapter 20 is interesting. By that time 'the days when a baron lived with his warriors on a mound overlooking a ditch lay far behind. Now he was a country gentleman, passed from one house to another, and enjoyed the amenity of parks and fish-ponds'.[144] Chapter 20 ordered trespassers upon enclosed private fish-ponds and parks to be imprisoned for three years, and then, if they could not pay their fines, to abjure the realm.

Imprisonment as a regular feature of British justice did not begin until the end of the sixteenth century when the vagrancy laws provided for the imprisonment of those who were idle or found wandering.[145] They were wandering, of course, because they had been turned out of their land-holdings. Having lost their homes, and the land which was their means of making a living, the public highways were the only places open to them, and crime the only source of income available to them. By Elizabeth's reign the problem had become explosive:

> The great floating population of vagabonds who used [the roads] presented a problem which could not be ignored. Here the need for action on a nation-wide scale was more than ever apparent, for in spite of all previous attempts to control the plague of beggars their number increased so greatly as to become a menace to public order ... There were no fewer than twenty-three categories of thieves and swindlers ... Such was the composition of this 'Merry England' that slept in hay lofts, sheepcotes, or on doorsteps, spreading terror in the country and disease in the towns.
>
> The official attitude to the whole fraternity of vagabonds had always been, and still was, one of fear-ridden ferocity: they were the true 'caterpillars of the commonwealth', who lick the sweat from the labourers' brows. But the impotent poor, the poor by casualty, who were 'poor in very deed', were acknowledged to be a charge on public benevolence.[146]

Here was the beginning of poor relief which four centuries later blossomed into the welfare state.

Decline of the Former Sanctions

Today the burden of private debt makes the old punishments impracticable. Building societies and banks as mortgagees have control of most of the private housing, and finance companies own many of the

---

144 Sir Maurice Powicke, *The Thirteenth Century*, Oxford University Press, 3rd edn, p.367.
145 See *Chambers Encyclopaedia*, Vol. 11, p.221a.
146 J.B. Black, *The Reign of Elizabeth*, Oxford, Clarendon Press, 2nd edn, 1959, pp.264-5.

expensive chattels provided under hire-purchase or leasing arrangements. The result is that the courts cannot forfeit the motor bikes, television sets or music centres of young offenders, or the houses and furniture of the more prosperous. Instead, over the last half century, expensive provision has been made to avoid imprisoning people, especially young people. They have instead been confined in Borstals, reform schools or detention centres (mild or tough), put on probation or into local authority care in hostels, or placed under the supervision of social workers. The cost is high. The taxpayer pays. Victims of crime have to be compensated too, but usually not by the criminal. Again the taxpayer pays, through the Criminal Injuries Compensation Board.

It makes matters worse that substantial fines are mostly used for punishing erring motorists. It causes resentment that they are treated more harshly than burglars. When real criminal offences are dealt with by fine, many Magistrates' Courts have to set aside one day's sitting each week for fine enforcement. They have to deal with defendants who have a number of small unpaid fines outstanding but often find it impossible to recover any substantial amount of the money due. At the trial there may have been witnesses giving enthusiastic evidence in favour of the defendant's good character but they are never called upon to write a cheque to keep their protégé out of prison. Their forefathers would have had to pledge money to end the threat of imprisonment.

It is possible to detect in early criminal law a principle that whoever belongs to a society is bound to abide by its rules. If he does not, he must lose the benefits the society affords. The ultimate sanction is expulsion. This is still the principle governing trade unions, clubs, learned societies, and the medical, legal and other professions.

Would not a new direction be given to the argument if more attention were paid to the ancient powers of the Sheriffs to seize and sell a criminal's chattels on behalf of the Crown? Hire-purchase companies would soon be refusing to lend to people with criminal records, who would in this limited sense become outlaws. How would public opinion react to this? Or to the idea that criminals (again as a kind of partial outlawry) should lose some or all of their entitlement to welfare benefits on conviction for multiple burglaries? The pendulum has swung between deterrence and reform, between education and punishment, but little notice has been taken of history as a guide to what could be done.

Parliament has the power to enact the necessary reforms, but history is never considered.

This sorry state of affairs makes it difficult to keep the peace in the national territory. The police force is pushed into a corner. A great deal of petty crime results from unemployment. It puts the courts in difficulty. Yet courts dare not fine to any satisfactory extent, that is to say, to show that justice is being done, because the level of welfare payments to the unemployed cannot stand it. So they resort to prison sentences.

In the eighteenth century, when criminals had got quite out of hand and highwaymen had achieved fame, excessive use of imprisonment by the courts, to get them out of the way, at length caused a surge of opinion in the nineteenth century in favour of prison reform. A hundred years later the courts were discouraged from sending people to prison, and the skills of sociologists were recruited to create a service to look after criminals and persuade them not to offend again. Sometimes the probation service was very successful in getting criminals into jobs, and young criminals into training colleges and universities. Unfortunately the place found for their 'client' was often at the expense of some respectable young man or woman. It is certainly not justice to take jobs or training opportunities from the law abiding in order to ease prison overcrowding. Sending criminals on holidays at public expense to stop them re-offending naturally causes an outcry against injustice.

In Search of Justice in Britain Today

JUSTICE CAN best be described as a situation where all is in order: everyone is in the right place, rendering what is due *from* him and receiving in return what is due *to* him. It is closely related to law and order, which stand under justice and support it. Justice is above them. *Justice* and *law* are connected by their common etymology. The root of justice (from Latin *jus, jungere*) is the same as that of the Greek ζευγος, ζευγμα, ζευγνυμι; Sanskrit √ *yu; yoga*. Like the English word *yoke*, all these words carry the meaning of 'joining together' or 'uniting'. It happens that *law* (from Latin *lex*, stem *leg-*, verbal form *ligere*) is similarly related to the meaning 'binding together', possibly cognate with Sanskrit √ *lig*. This makes it cognate also with *religion*, which modern etymologists derive from the Latin *religare*.[147] In Blackstone's phrase concerning natural law, justice depends on such laws as 'existed in the nature of things antecedent to any positive precept, namely the eternal, immutable laws of good and evil, to which the Creator himself conforms'.[148] Only Truth, the Absolute, is above justice. It is the source of justice.

It has to be said that justice is not easy to find in the government of nations of the world today. In Britain we are more fortunate than most. Our defence against tyranny is found in such mechanisms as the jury system and the common law doctrine of habeas corpus, now firmly established by statutes (of 1679, 1816 and 1862), although both these safeguards are now under attack from Europe. We also have an independent judiciary, although this too may not last if we adopt too much of the European system. We have freedom of speech – to the extent that it is not stifled by the fashion (so effective that it is almost tyrannical) of 'political correctness'. Yet some of our laws have put society out of joint.

The Family

The right place for children is in the family. Their law should be from the head of the family, and enforced by him or her. In many of today's splintered families children are in the hands of social workers, some in the care of the courts, a few even having to litigate against their parents. In many cases schools have become child-minders for couples who both work and who between them have insufficient time to look after their offspring. The effect on literacy and numeracy is startling, but the efforts to overcome it by compulsory education force many children, who are by nature more suited to practical pursuits than academic learning, to stay at school beyond the age that suits their talents. Many would be far better employed elsewhere. They suffer from the political shibboleth of 'equality' because the Education Acts, in common with other statutory enactments, lay down one rule for all, disregarding the natural differences between individual children.

---

147 Cicero and other ancient writers derived *religio* from *relegere* ('to collect together'), which would fit in well with our idea of Christ as the good shepherd. But modern etymologists mostly reject Cicero on this point. Nearly all of the information in this paragraph is conveniently to be found in Lewis and Short's *Latin Dictionary*, under 'Jus'.
148 See fuller quotation from Blackstone *supra*, pp.46-7.

Classes

Today the very mention of 'classes' sends a *frisson* of distaste down the spine. The classless society is regarded as a desirable end in itself.

In 1962 the head of the Shankara tradition[149] said, in answer to a question on the four castes, that 'the fourfold system of Manu is not only for man; it is in everything living – in vegetation, in animals, in minerals'. We tend to be repelled today by any mention of division into classes, but if it accords with natural law we have much to learn if we try rigidly to impose something different on account of political correctness.

Law

Law should be the means of keeping the peace and deciding conflicts between individuals, but oppressive and unjust regulations frequently override the common law. The system of legal aid, by which access to the courts is now gained, is only too often a system of blackmail. It forces the unaided party, who will have to pay the cost of the case whether he wins or loses, to settle for any sum that will save him the huge cost of litigation. From parliament, from powers deputed to ministers or quangos, and now from the European Union, come a constant shower of instructions having the force of law, which interfere in every walk of life. The tangle of regulations brings us no nearer to justice. The complication is immense. How can the revered precept that 'ignorance of the law is no excuse' be preserved when laws no longer accord with the natural feeling for justice in the heart of the average man?

The old Anglo-Saxon law codes were collections of the important customs that good people already observed, issued in the name of the king. These customs became the common law enshrined in the Laws of Ine, the Laws of Alfred, the Laws of Athelstan and so on. They so obviously accorded with the common outlook of their time that ignorance of the law was in truth no excuse. Contrast this with endless regulations from Brussels and Whitehall consisting of whatever an ever-increasing bureaucracy cares to devise, either because they think it good for us or because they must appease some pressure group which may threaten their power. Their regulations in no way reflect the common sense of the law-abiding, and can be adhered to only after tedious study.

---

149 His Holiness Shantanand Saraswati Shankaracharya of North India, 1953-81. He died in 1997.

The Economy

Of all our institutions the economy is perhaps the most lacking in justice. People differ by nature, but on a scale which, in height for example, is measured in a small range of inches or centimetres. By contrast the ever-widening gap between the incomes of rich and poor now has to be measured in many millions of pounds. It clearly bears no natural relationship to the real differences between human beings. The injustice of it is compounded by the extent to which the very rich can avoid paying income tax on the bulk of their income. It cannot be effectively controlled. Its success depends on the degree of expertise the rich can command. Income tax is the most obvious direct tax, but governments do not like to be seen to be increasing it. Instead they raise the level of taxation by increasing indirect taxes hidden in prices, which hits the unsuspecting poor more even than the moderately well-off.[150] Far from dealing with these abuses, which are fundamental to the quality of life, parliament concerns itself with trivialities.

Politics

This concern for trivialities is not lost on the discerning public. Respect for our legislators is lower than it has ever been. Scandal and 'sleaze' in political circles is the usual diet of the newspapers. Television has taken hold of people in all ranks of life, encouraging skin-deep sentimentality, with life portrayed as a 'sit-com' and with rock stars, football players and 'personalities' of every kind used to maintain the viewing figures and the profits. They dominate commercial television: cultivated with obsequious flattery, they are invited to pronounce upon matters of public importance. Publicly funded television tries to compete by reducing serious investigation and argument. On all sides the search is on for the popular, superficial, easily absorbed soundbite. Politics is seen by most to consist of seeking popularity in order to retain power and privilege. Elections are decided on personalities not policies, and political philosophies are almost non-existent. Indeed, there is now little fundamental distinction between the parties. Statesmanship is nowhere to be found.

---

150 *Social Trends* in 1998 showed that indirect taxes as a percentage of disposable income were 31% for those in the lowest fifth of households, while the highest fifth paid 16%. This demonstrates how indirect taxation bears hardest on the poor, although the trade unions usually succeed in keeping up the expected standard of living of the wage-earner. When that happens, the employer is further mulcted in tax through the wages he pays his employees.

Political Ineptitude

Governments of all complexions devote their time to alleviating symptoms instead of seeking a cure. By neglecting their duty to see that every family enjoys its share in the national territory, a culture of crime and drugs grows up, chiefly affecting the idle. Although most are idle because of poverty and the inability to find work, some are idle through excessive wealth, the lack of the need to work for a living. Boredom in both cases is an incentive to crime and drugs. The culture of wage-slavery is similarly derived from the inability to work freely, making it essential to 'get a job'. Yet only some of the population are suited by nature to service. Accordingly, those driven by adverse circumstances to find a job become square pegs in round holes, often overworked, unhappy and sometimes even suffering in health as a result. Service has come to be looked upon as degrading. Formerly it was a matter of pride. Litigation between master and servant (to use terminology now banished as politically incorrect) grows apace. Special courts (employment tribunals) have been set up to deal with it. It has even become dangerous for small firms to take on servants because they can so easily find a grouse on which to litigate.

The expense of looking after criminals in and out of jail is large, but when added to the cost of the rest of the welfare state, including the health service, the cost is formidable. To pay for it the armed forces of the Crown are reduced below the limit of safety. They are insufficient to support the popular foreign policy of restraining governments in various parts of the world from massacring their fellow citizens who differ from them in race, religion, or simply in policy. So tyrants are condemned by much rhetoric but rarely confronted with force, unless it be by bombing from a safe height. This is the result of government failure truly to protect the national territory and all the people in it.

As to order, the chaos on the roads and railways, and at airports, with so many rushing anxiously to keep up with the pace of life, and suffering the tedium of late arrivals and departures, betokens a major flaw in the shape of society. People tend to live long distances from their work, and have to travel even longer distances to find rest in peace and quiet for weekends and holidays. Such people are simply not in the right place. This is partly due to their having to find employment in order to make a living, and, as wage slaves, feeling the need to flee to a far-off home or resort to recoup their spirit and retain their sanity.

Justice is not a question simply of righting wrongs. The tale is told of the agitator for justice who, once he was given a new pair of boots, was content with the state of affairs. The trouble was that he could only consider justice from his own particular point of view. The greatest enemy of justice is the ego, which is a sin besetting all human kind.

The modern view is usually that human beings are essentially good, that only a little gentle persuasion is necessary to make them perfect.[151] Only perpetrators of genocide, torture and serious sexual offences (especially against children) can be condemned outright. This is a travesty of the truth; it renders government today incapable of dealing with ordinary human folly and wickedness. History at least teaches the unchanging horror of human behaviour. Jerusalem, sacked by Nebuchadnezzar in 586 BC, by the Romans in AD 70 and by the Crusaders in 1099, illustrates a continuing policy of extermination surpassed only by Joshua when he 'utterly destroyed all that was in the city of Jericho, both man and woman, young and old, and ox, and sheep, and ass, with the edge of the sword'. History abounds with such horrors, including the massacres of their own compatriots by Chairman Mao, Stalin and Hitler. The struggle between human good and evil lacks a built-in moral or spiritual compass. Advance towards justice requires discipline and guidance from an objective external point of reference.

Beauty and the Beast

It would be easy to list the irritations in everyday life which make people despair of present-day Britain and the list would be long. It would cover Church and State, religion, philosophy, politics and economics, wealth and poverty, freedom stifled by regulation, the arts, the sciences, the professions, especially the clerical, medical and legal professions, and many other sections of our society. Crime and the inadequacy of its punishment sicken the law-abiding, as do prisons overcrowded with people who should be at work, and an army of well-intentioned sociologists taking on the daunting task of looking after criminals whom the courts can find no suitable way of punishing. In short, we live in a world

---

151 Much of this paragraph is prompted by Edward Norman's weekly column in the *Daily Telegraph*.

where the remarkable beauty and order of nature contrasts with a remarkable disorder and ugliness in human kind. Litter in the streets and old furniture and vehicles dumped on spare ground betoken this disorder. If the centre of a town or city is beautiful, away from the centre there are usually dreary suburbs, and drab slums. Outside in the streets ill-dressed crowds have no pride in their appearance; they pass by with unseeing eyes and unhearing ears. People collecting welfare benefits swell Post Office queues, because they are prevented from working by our curious laws. Many who crowd doctors' surgeries are not really ill, while the hard-working who are ill cannot afford the time to join the long queue for a consultation.

Disintegration

Britain, formerly Great Britain, now has many levels of government. The most important are the three and a half 'central' parliamentary governments, English, Scottish, Welsh and, in half-baked form, Northern Irish. Above these, European government has overriding sovereignty in a large number of important respects in all four countries. Below them are county and district governments with considerable powers. Only time will tell how this confused situation will resolve itself, and which of the four peoples, or which combination of any of them, will come within the definition of a nation. They are all united by language and they share a great deal of history, but no one can yet tell how far their cultures will divide them. Nor is it clear how separate they will make their territory. The admission, particularly into England, of immigrants of all colours, creeds and cultures, without ensuring that they adapt to the basics of our way of life, and learn our language at least as a second language, makes nationality a difficult concept.[152]

'Just People'

What the foregoing list of irritations displays is a society that is disintegrating. The truth, however, is a good deal more simple than a long list of irritations would suggest. Society has within it many kinds of associations of people bound together by a common interest –

---

152 Central government and some local authorities in England send their various circulars out in a number of Indian and African languages. In some cases the number of 'ethnic' families in the locality is very small indeed, but the expense of translators and printing for this tiny minority is still undertaken.

political, medical, legal, philosophical, literary, commercial, recreational and so on. Overall it consists of families. An essential feature of justice is for laws to set the parts in proper order in relation to each other and to the whole. Our prime need is for integration, in society as a whole, in the many associations within it, and in its constituent individual families. This is only possible when individuals love justice, and seek first to establish it in their own lives and then, within the limits of their powers, in the institutions large or small to which they belong. The need is for the 'just man', 'just people', even more than for justice. This Platonic conception that the macrocosm reflects the microcosm is still understood by people of good sense.

Religion
Guidance ought to be available from religion. This can only safely be discovered by study of the Scriptures, with such aid as scholarship can provide. In this regard it is unfortunate that the Greek words used by Plato for *the just* and *justice*[153] when they occur in the Bible are usually translated as *the righteous*, and *righteousness*. These words have changed their meaning: *righteousness* now smacks of the self-righteous. To be called righteous today might almost be regarded as defamatory!

However, Christ's warning against the false messiahs who were bound to come, and have indeed come at various times, applies to all religions. Even before Christianity became the recognised religion of the Roman Empire, the teaching of Christ, whose birth the year 2000 was supposed to celebrate, had been made the property of institutions, each of which declared its own version to be the only true version. It is in the nature of institutions to take on a corporate identity, and an ego to express that identity. Christianity has been used to boost the egos of these institutions. After centuries of bitter feuding over 'heresies', in the eleventh century a schism occurred between Western Catholic and Eastern Orthodox Christianity chiefly over the doctrine of trinity. When the seed of the renaissance, slow in growth, blossomed in the sixteenth century, and the scientific age began in the seventeenth, Christianity was under threat. In the eighteenth century the French Revolution swamped Christianity in

---

153 δικαιος and δικαιοσυνη.

France, and the publication of *The Origin of Species* in 1859 helped to spread the flood of atheism throughout the Western world.

Meanwhile the Western Church had split into Catholics and Protestants, with sub-divisions especially prevalent among Protestant sects, some of which divided again and again into sub-sects. In the twentieth century a contrary movement of ecumenism became the fashion in debate, but splintering continued. Our last millennium celebrations were almost entirely secular. As the two thousandth anniversary of the birth of Christ almost certainly occurred in the year 1996, it is possible to regard it as a blessing that these celebrations were four years too late. What emanates from various churches nowadays as Christ's doctrine is often a travesty of the true mystery of its meaning.

The Old Covenant

The first five books of the Old Covenant,[154] known as the Pentateuch, contain the Torah (the Law), and the Covenant with God. If the people chose to obey the law, then God promised in return to make them a prosperous nation, and to give them a land in which to dwell. The editors of the Jerusalem Bible remark: 'The Promise, the Choice, the Covenant, the Law – these are the golden threads, the warp and woof of the Pentateuch.'[155]

The Three Religions

It is a remarkable fact that, in spite of the hostility often displayed between them, Judaism, Christianity and Islam share and ultimately depend upon the teaching contained in the Law and the Prophets of the Hebrews.

To the Jews, of course, these, together with the Psalms, *are* the scriptures. As to Christianity, Christ himself said he had come to fulfil the law and the prophets, and of the Torah, which is by far the most important part of them. He added:

---

154 This is the correct translation of the Greek word διαθηκη, and until the beginning of the second century AD the sacred books of the Jews were known to Christians as the Old Covenant. Unfortunately, when the Greek Bibles were translated into Latin, διαθηκη was taken in its classical Greek meaning of 'last will and testament'. Consequently, the Old Covenant was dubbed *Vetus Testamentum*, and this led to the Christian parts being called *Novum Testamentum*. Modern translations of the Bible have rightly substituted 'covenant' for the word 'testament' wherever it occurs in the text, but in spite of these amendments the two parts of the Bible still continue, erroneously, to be referred to as the New and Old Testaments.

155 *The Jerusalem Bible*, Introduction, p.13.

Verily, verily, I say unto you [He could not have been more emphatic than that], till heaven and earth pass, one jot or one tittle shall in no wise pass from the law, till all be fulfilled.[156]

As to Islam, A.J. Arberry, Oxford's former Professor of Arabic, in the introduction to his translation of the Koran says:

Many passages state that the Koran had been sent down 'confirming what was before it', by which was meant the Torah and the Christian gospels. The content of the Jewish and Christian scriptures, excepting such falsifications as had been introduced into them, were taken as true and known.

There is one portion of the Torah which, were it taken seriously by the teachers of all three of these religions, would put an end to much of the animosity between them. Underlying the whole of the Torah is the warning that God gave to Moses in the desert at Sinai:

The land shall not be sold for ever [*in perpetuity* in the Authorised Version]: for the land is mine; for ye are strangers and sojourners with me [*settlers, tenants* or *guests* in other translations].[157]

On this verse, former Chief Rabbi Dr J.H. Hertz commented:

This verse enunciates the basic principle upon which all these enactments [of the Torah] rest. 'The earth is the Lord's' (Psalm 24:1), and His people hold their lands in fee from Him. The ground itself, then, was not a proper object of sale, but only the result of man's labour on the ground.[158]

Dr Hertz, a noted biblical scholar, is by no means alone among Rabbis in this. The Christian Church, possibly because they are, or at any rate were, extensive landowners have rather avoided referring to it.

Moses on Mount Sinai, and Joshua during the campaign to conquer the promised land, had been more than once instructed by God to share the land equably between families:

Ye shall dispossess the inhabitants of the land, and dwell therein: for I have given you the land to possess it. And ye shall divide the land by lot for an inheritance [Greek *kataklêronomêsete*] among your families: and to the more ye shall give the more inheritance, and to the fewer ye shall give the less inheritance.[159]

---

156 Matthew 5:18, amongst the beatitudes. Also in Luke 16:18, a chapter concerned with poverty, where a similar warning was given specifically to the Pharisees.
157 Leviticus 25:23.
158 Dr J.H. Hertz (d.1946), *The Pentateuch and Haftorahs*, London, Soncino Press, 2nd edn, 1937, p.534.
159 Numbers 33:53-4. Cf. also Numbers 26:55-6, Joshua 13:6, Numbers 34:13 and other references where this same instruction was repeated in slightly different form.

Yet, however equitably the land is divided initially, changes inevitably occur in the course of a generation or two. Some families will have grown larger, others will have declined in number. Some will have suffered crop failures or loss of animals through storm, drought, disease, war and other calamities, and many will have been forced into slavery through debt. In order to re-establish the inheritance after such changes, and prevent a return to the Egyptian servitude, the Torah ordained a *jubilee* – 'the Acceptable Year of the Lord' – which would stop land falling into the hands of those who could thereby enrich themselves and oppress the poor. Accordingly, Leviticus Chapter 25 lays down:

> Every seven Sabbaths of years ... shall be unto thee forty and nine years. Then shalt thou cause the trumpet of the jubile [*sic*] to sound ... throughout all your land. And ye shall hallow the fiftieth year, and proclaim *liberty throughout all the land* unto all the inhabitants thereof; it shall be a jubile unto you; and ye shall return every man unto his possession and ye shall return every man unto his family.

In short, when the trumpet of the jubilee sounds, all debts are cancelled and all slaves set free, and all lands that had been sold are returned. A sale amounted in practice to a lease till jubilee, when it would be returned to the original family. Liberty, and return to the family inheritance, is the substance of the jubilee.[160]

Poverty

In the centuries after Moses the jubilee seems to have gone many times by default, causing the prophets to rail against the way the upper classes treated the poor. The most famous passage is in Isaiah 3:14:

> The Lord will enter into judgement with the ancients of his people, and the princes thereof: for ye have eaten up the vineyard, the spoil of the poor is in your houses. What mean ye that ye beat my people to pieces, and grind the faces of the poor? saith the Lord God of Hosts.

There are many similar condemnations of the oppression of the poor in the Psalms and the other prophets.[161] Christ himself declared 'Woe'

---

160 In AD 1300 Pope Boniface VIII instituted a jubilee in which special indulgence was granted to Catholics who visited Rome and fulfilled certain conditions, visiting shrines etc. It produced a considerable income for the Holy See.

161 Psalms 10:8, 35:10, Isaiah 5:8, 3:14 and Micah *passim*, including 2:2: 'they covet fields, and take them by violence; and houses, and take them away so they oppress a man and his house, even a man and his heritage'(Luke 20:47).

unto the hypocritical establishment of his day: 'for ye devour widows' houses, and for a pretence make long prayer: therefore ye shall receive the greater damnation'.[162]

In the Synagogue at Nazareth[163]

Christ reminded the Galileans of the jubilee. 'There was delivered unto him the book of the prophet Isaiah, and he opened it and found the place (it was chapter 61:1):

> The Spirit of the Lord is upon me, because he hath anointed me to preach the *gospel to the poor*; he hath sent me to heal the broken-hearted, to preach deliverance to the captives, and recovering of sight to the blind, to set at liberty them that are bruised, to preach the Acceptable Year of the Lord ... And he closed the book and gave it again unto the minister ...

Jesus stopped the quotation at this point abruptly, indeed dramatically, in mid-sentence. The complete sentence in the Hebrew would have been 'to preach the acceptable year of the Lord, *and the day of vengeance of our God'*. But 'the day of vengeance of our God' would become relevant only if they rejected Christ's teaching. They did reject it, and it remains rejected today.

Although at first 'all bare him witness and wondered at the gracious words which proceeded out of his mouth', this favourable reception did not last. Those who heard him in the synagogue were ultimately (verse 28) filled with wrath. They thrust him out of the city and led him to the brow of the hill on which the city stood, that they might cast him down headlong. But he, passing through them, went his way. Why such fury? The gospel (or glad tidings) to the poor, the Acceptable Year of the Lord, the jubilee, was probably seen as a direct attack on the propertied classes.

The essential requirement of the Torah is that the land be recognised as belonging to God, not to any private individual. 'The Earth is the Lord's, and the fullness thereof.'[164] 'The fullness thereof' is indeed the divine providence for the support of the whole of mankind. In every nation, a *share* in the national territory is the lawful inheritance of each family. If there is to be plenty for all, it must be kept shared.

---

162 Matthew 23:14, Mark 12:40 and Luke 20:47.
163 Luke 4:16ff.
164 Psalm 24:1.

Under the true rule of law, the rule of God ('Thy Kingdom come'), there can be no landlessness and therefore no poverty, no oppression, no bondage. The people are free because they enjoy the means of subsistence given them by God and, except for those crippled in body or mind, can by their own labour support themselves in all the necessities of life.

Conclusion

ALL SYSTEMS have to be kept in balance. There has to be an equilibrium. This is well understood by those who study nature. It is also true of man-made systems. An electrical system needs earthing, a hydraulic system needs provision for overflow, a railway needs sidings to take from and give to a railway the stock it needs as rush hours alternate with slack periods. A gas central heating system needs a balanced flue and an expansion water tank. Sieves and filters carry off waste. Milton spoke of 'the pendulous round Earth, with balanced air in counterpoise'. All these make one wonder what happens to keep human kind in equilibrium in relation to justice. We do not know. We can only set out the hints given by various sources. These reveal a divergence as to the nature of time. Is time linear or circular? Are the moments of time arranged as round the face of a traditional clock or along a straight line as in a digital timepiece?

The Real Law

The theme in a number of psalms is that, overall, contrary to popular belief, virtue *is* rewarded, the unjust do *not* have the best of it:

> I have seen the wicked in great power, and flourishing like the green bay tree. Yet he passed away, and, lo, he was not. Mark the perfect man, and behold the upright: for the end of that man is peace. But the transgressors shall be destroyed together: the end of the wicked shall be cut off. [Psalm 37:35-8]

> Lord, thou hast been our dwelling place in all generations ... Thou turnest man to destruction; and sayest, Return ye children of men. For a thousand years in thy sight are but as yesterday when it is past, and as a watch in the night. [Psalm 90:1, 3]

> For Thine is the kingdom, the power, and the glory... for ever ... and ever.

As already mentioned, Pythagoras taught the transmigration of souls. According to the Jewish historian Josephus, this was also the doctrine of the Pharisees.[165] It is to be found in the Kabbalah. It has been the firm belief of the Jewish Kairites, who claim to be heirs of the tradition of the Essenes. It was espoused by some of the fathers of the early Church, especially Origen (?185-284) and Eusebius (264-340). St Jerome (d. 420) affirmed that it was also propounded among the early Christians as an esoteric and traditional doctrine which was entrusted to the select few.[166] The only scriptural authority for it seems to be in the word παλιγγενησις, which the Authorised Version translates as *regeneration*.[167] P.D. Ouspensky points out that it is translated as *wiedergeburt* (rebirth) in German, and by a word of similar meaning in the Russian Bible. This would certainly be its meaning in classical Greek: born over again. In India it is common to the various sects following Vedanta, and to Buddhism. Plato and the Neo-Platonists taught it. The doctrine takes different forms in these and other systems.

Transmigration was, however, implicitly condemned by the Western Church at the Councils of Lyons (1274) and Florence (1439), which declared that souls go immediately after death to heaven, hell or purgatory. This certainly discourages the apathy and idleness which may arise from supposing that the next life will afford yet another chance of improvement. But it sits uncomfortably in a universe in which repetitive turning is the norm – the earth on its own axis, the moon round the earth, the earth round the sun and so on. Given the remarkable cyclic processes of nature – for example, spring, summer, autumn, winter and then spring again – it would not be surprising if some who 'profess and call themselves Christians' held a similar belief. It is possible that a substantial minority of Christians have done so even in modern times.[168] It makes it easier to say, in the Apostles' Creed, 'I believe in the resurrection of the body, and the life everlasting,' or, in the Nicene Creed, 'I look for the resurrection of the dead and the life of the world to come.'

Without transmigration the orthodoxy of Western Christianity does not provide a morally satisfying explanation of the inequalities of fortune among mankind. P.D. Ouspensky[169] quotes Simplicius (fl. *c*.530),

---

165 Josephus, *Antiquities of the Jews*, xviii, 1, 3 and *The Jewish War*, ii, 8, 14.
166 Christian D. Ginsburg, *The Kabbalah*, 1865; London, Routledge, 1920, p.125, note 23.
167 Mattthew 19:28 and Titus 3:5.
168 This rather bold statement is based only on the author's (possibly faulty) recollection of a newspaper report of a survey forty or fifty years ago which indicated this to be the case.
169 P.D. Ouspensky, *A New Model of the Universe*, London, Arkana, 1984, Chapter xi, p.468.

who had access to the library of the Platonic Academy in Athens until its closure in AD 529:

> The Pythagoreans said that the same things are repeated again and again. In this connection it is interesting to note the words of Eudemus, Aristotle's disciple: Some people accept and some deny that time repeats itself. Repetition is understood in different senses. One kind of repetition may be in the natural order of things, like repetition of summers and winters and other seasons ... But if we are to believe the Pythagoreans there is another type of repetition. That means that I shall talk to you and sit exactly like this and I shall have in my hand the same stick, and everything will be the same as it is now, and time, as it can be supposed, will be the same. Because if movements (of heavenly bodies) and many other things are the same, what occurred before and what will occur afterwards are also the same. This applies also to repetition, which is always the same. Everything is the same and therefore time is the same.

If heaven, hell and purgatory are taken to be aspects of what we have to undergo at different times in this present life, then the orthodoxy of Lyons and Florence would blend well with the idea of eternal recurrence expressed by the Pythagoreans.

But the controversy has not been resolved. As Shakespeare put it in one of his deeply religious sonnets (Sonnet 53):

> If there be nothing new, but that which is,
> Hath been before, how are our minds beguiled,
> Which, labouring for invention, bear amiss
> The second burthen of a former child.

The Myth of Er

Towards the end of Plato's *Republic* Socrates, after a long dialectical discourse, had succeeded in demonstrating to his friends the truth that the just man is rewarded at the hands of gods and men in his lifetime, in addition to the blessings which come simply from being just. He then went on to say that 'these rewards of virtue are as nothing, when compared with the rewards awaiting the just after death', and to explain this mystical statement he concluded the dialogue by relating the famous Myth of Er.[170]

Er was killed in battle but, when his body was about to be cremated some days later, he came to life again and was able to relate what he had

---

170 The following précis is taken largely from Cornford's translation of Plato's *Republic*.

seen in the other world. He described a marvellous place where, in the sky above, were two openings, one leading to heaven, the other from heaven; and below in the earth were two similar openings leading to and from Hades. Between them sat judges who, after sentence was given, sent the just to heaven above and the unjust below, each with a placard bearing evidence of his deeds. Each batch of travel-stained arrivals from below, and clean and bright arrivals from above, seemed glad to turn aside in the meadow, where they camped like pilgrims at a festival and questioned each other about what had happened to them in the world above or below. The upshot was this. For every wrong they had done, and for anyone they had injured, they had to pay the penalty ten times over, while deeds of kindness and justice in life were rewarded in the same measure. When the tyrant Ardiaeus the Great (the Hitler or Stalin of his time) tried to emerge from below they saw him stopped, bound hand and foot, subjected to all kinds of harsh treatment and slung back below. They were told he would never come back again.

After spending seven days in the encampment, the company were escorted to the place where they would choose their next life. There they saw the 'Spindle of Necessity' like a great pillar of light turning eight circular basin-shaped whorls carrying the fixed stars, the sun, the moon, the planets and the earth in their several directions. This model of the universe rested on the knees of Necessity while her three daughters, the Fates governing Past, Present and Future, sat on three thrones placed equidistantly round it, and helped each other to keep the whorls turning in constant motion. Upon each of the eight circular whorls stood a siren, each chanting 'a continuous note, so that all the eight notes made up the harmonies of a single scale'.

The souls were then all set to choose their new lives. Having drawn lots as to who should choose first, one by one they examined the lives scattered on the ground before them. The lives were of all living creatures. Orpheus chose the life of a swan and a well-known singer that of a nightingale, the choices being governed by the habits of their former lives. Some chose wealth, some power. The last to choose was the famous 'wily Odysseus' who spent a long time searching for a life of quiet obscurity in order to avoid a repetition of the troubles he had already suffered. Finding this life at last, neglected by the rest, he chose it gladly.

Here it seems, my dear Glaucon, a man's whole fortunes are at stake. On this account each one of us should lay aside all other learning, to study only how he may discover one who can give him the knowledge enabling him to distinguish the good life from the evil, and always and everywhere to choose the best within his reach ... All else he will leave out of account; for, as we have seen, this is the supreme choice for a man, both while he lives and after death.

Finally, all journeyed through stifling heat to the river of forgetfulness called Lethe, where they were made to drink the waters which, save for those few who have the wisdom to drink no more than they must, make men forget everything. Then they fell asleep. At midnight there was thunder and an earthquake, and they were carried up this way and that to their birth, like shooting stars.

And so, Glaucon, the tale was preserved, and if we will listen, it may save us, and all will be well when we cross the river of *Lethe*, and will keep our souls unspotted from the world. But if you believe me that the soul is immortal and able to endure the extremes of good and evil, we shall always hold to the upward path, in all things pursuing Justice with the help of Wisdom. Then we shall be at peace with the gods and with ourselves, both in this world and when, like winners in the Games, we receive our prize; and so not only here, but in the long thousand-year journey which I have described, ευ πραττω-μεν – 'we shall fare well'.

Plato's conclusion more than two thousand years ago was that an enduring justice is found only when just men and women follow and uphold the highest principles and natural law of human conduct as their Creator intended. How could there be ethnic cleansing or abject poverty in a world that truly practised 'Love thy neighbour as thyself'? Of course, a brief moment of justice may be achieved by a fair judgement in a court of law, a proper sentence for the guilty, or a much needed reform. How much better if justice could be a way of life?

The work lies ahead for each of us.

Appendix

IN *Udale v Bloomsbury Area Health Authority*,[1] the mother, following a failed sterilisation operation, sought compensation for the cost of bringing up the child who was born healthy and normal. Sir Kenneth Jupp explained his reasons for declining to grant damages as follows:

'The considerations that particularly impress me are the following: (1) It is highly undesirable that any child should learn that a court has publicly declared his life or birth to be a mistake, a disaster even, and that he or she is unwanted or rejected. Such pronouncements would disrupt families and weaken the structure of society. (2) A plaintiff such as Mrs Udale would get little or no damages because her love and care for her child and her joy, ultimately, at his birth would be set off against and might cancel out the inconvenience and financial disadvantages which naturally accompany parenthood. By contrast, a plaintiff who nurtures bitterness in her heart and refused to let her maternal instinct take over would be entitled to large damages. In short virtue would go unrewarded; unnatural rejection of womanhood and motherhood would be generously compensated. This, in my judgment, cannot be just. (3) Medical men would be under subconscious pressure to encourage abortions in order to avoid claims for medical negligence which would arise if the child were allowed to be born. (4) It has been the assumption of our culture from time immemorial that a child coming into the world, even if, as some say, "the world is a vale of tears", is a blessing and an occasion for rejoicing.'

In other cases on similar lines the Court of Appeal did not support his judgment; but in *McFarlane v Tayside Health Board*[2] the House of Lords adopted his reasoning and said that that was the law. Lawyers accept the wisdom and the care which Sir Kenneth Jupp showed in his choice of words.

1 [1983] 2 All ER 522.
2 [1999] 3 WLR 1301.

Index